Table of Contents

We are deeply grateful to our friend Bill Hamlin for his help and patience. His perspective and knowledge of compound-specific maintenance procedures was invaluable in making this a complete volume. Thank you, Bill.

We also wish to thank our friend Gerald Taylor. While he did not directly contribute to this volume, he has been our technical mentor for many years. Without Gerald's help, our technical skills and knowledge would not be what they are today.

Introduction

Equipment maintenance is an important but often neglected aspect of archery. Having equipment in tip-top shape means you're ready for shooting, whether for recreation, hunting, or competition. It also means you know you'll be shooting with equipment that is safe and reliable.

So why is maintenance neglected? The main reason is because, prior to this book, there were few readily available sources for this kind of information. Many skills have been passed from person to person – if anyone is around to help. That's what prompted us to write this book.

In these pages you'll find a compilation of common procedures important to archers, regardless of shooting style. Whether you shoot a compound, recurve, or even a traditional bow, there's something for you in this book. Clear illustrations augment the text and help you master each procedure. Each Chapter also has the necessary background material, so you can make better decisions about what to do before starting.

To get the most from this book we suggest reading through the procedure thoroughly first. One procedure may reference another, so reading ahead keeps you from having to stop and back up to learn another procedure to complete the task at hand.

Maintaining your equipment can be enjoyable, save money and give you confidence in your shooting and equipment that you've never had before. As you master the techniques in this book, you gain a valuable skills you'll use often as you enjoy the sport of archery.

It's our pleasure to be a part of your learning experience…welcome to archery maintenance!

Part I: Working with Arrows

The procedures in this section describe how to repair arrows or build a new set, whether you are a hunter or competition target shooter, compound or recurve archer.

Chapter 1: Installing and Replacing Nocks – Broken nocks can be easily replaced, keeping your arrows in good condition.

Chapter 2: Fletching Arrows – Fletching may get damaged when shooting. When building arrows, they must be fletched.

Chapter 3: Cutting Arrows – This allows you to set the correct arrow length when building new arrows or shorten existing ones.

Chapter 4: Installing and Replacing Points – Damaged or missing points must be replaced and new arrows require points be installed.

Chapter 5: Checking Arrows – Periodically all arrows need to be checked to be sure they are straight and the carbon is intact.

Chapter 1
Installing and Replacing Nocks

There are two times when you need to work with nocks – when either replacing a damaged nock or building a new set of of arrows. Installing or replacing a nock is easy. First, some thoughts on nocks.

- If you are considering purchasing a used set of arrows, don't let damaged nocks be a reason to reject buying an otherwise good set. If you damage or lose a nock, there is no reason to discard the arrow; simply replace the nock.

- When preparing new arrows, use the correct nock size. Match the size, brand, and color when replacing a nock, especially if you are considering competition. Tournament rules require arrows be identical.

- Nocks can be purchased at most archery stores, but nocks for higher-quality target arrows may be difficult to get locally. When purchasing nocks it is important to know the arrow specifications (shaft size and brand). If you're new to archery, take an arrow with a good nock with you; it insures you get the same ones.

- Some nocks for tournament arrows have a choice of two throat sizes (where the string sits), allowing a better fit on different string thicknesses. When purchasing a new set, make sure the nock fits the on the string easily.

There are five general types of nocks. Determine the type you have, then read the information on how to install or replace it. But first determine the nock alignment. It is different for finger and release shooters, regardless of the type of bow used.

Nock Alignment

The nock must be aligned with one fletching – called the index fletching. The Index fletching may all be the same color as the rest of the fletching, or it may be a different color. If the index fletching is a different color, the nock is aligned to it.

Most nocks have a small raised nib or ridge on one side. This is an index and should be aligned with the index fletching. Feeling the nib with your fingers, you can nock the arrow on the string in proper alignment without looking at it.

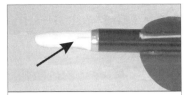

The index nib on a nock. This should be lined up with the index fletching.

The alignment is different for a release and a finger shooter because of the type of arrrow rest each needs.

Nock Alignment for Release Shooters – Almost always the rest used with a release is a launcher. Typically, the index fletching points either straight up or down, parallel with the string. The slot in the nock should be in line (parallel) with the index fletching.

Nock Alignment for Finger Shooters – Finger shooters, whether compound or recurve, use a rest and a pressure button or some other type of pressure point. For this arrangement, the nock slot is perpendicular to the index fletchting so the other two fletchings have the greatest clearance as the arrow passes the bow.

When replacing a nock, align the nock so it matches the others. All arrows in a set should have the same nock alignment.

Nock alignment for single-piece launchers that have a V notch or narrow bend on which the arrow sits.

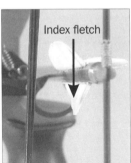

Nock alignment for launchers with either a fork or a gap that allows the index fletching to pass.

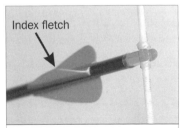

Nock alignment for finger shooters. The slot of the nock is perpendicular to the index fletching.

Nocks that Insert Directly into the Arrow Shaft

These nocks have a piece that goes directly into the end of the arrow shaft. The nock is held in place by the friction of the insert against the inside of the arrow shaft. No glue is required.

Removing the Damaged Nock – Remove the damaged nock by pulling it out. If the fit is too tight to remove with your fingers, use pliers, but be sure to grasp only the nock. Pull the nock straight out, rotating it if necessary.

Installing the New Nock – Push/slide the new nock into the end of the arrow shaft. It may help to twist it slightly while pushing. When it is fully seated, align the nock with the fletching.

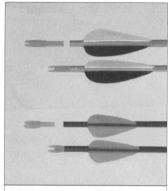

Nocks that insert directly into the arrow shaft.

Nocks with an Adapter

Adapters are a small machined aluminum pieces inserted into the back end of the arrow to make the nock fit. This is common on large diameter arrows or to make a small nock fit a larger arrow shaft.

No glue is needed for the nock because it is held in place by the pressure of the nock against the adapter. Depending on the fit of the adapter in the end of the arrow shaft, the adapter may or my not be glued in place. If it is glued, a low-temperature hot melt glue should be used.

Removing the Damaged Nock – Remove the nock by carefully pulling it straight out of the arrow shaft. The adapter sometimes comes out with the nock, too. If this happens, you may

Nocks with an adapter. The adapter is the silver piece on the end of the arrow shaft. It makes the nock fit the arrow.

have to replace the adapter along with the nock, as getting the adapter off the nock can easily distort it, making it unusable.

If the adapter remained in the arrow shaft, evaluate its condition before replacing the nock. If it is damaged in any way, it must be replaced, too. To remove the adapter, first determine if it was glued in. If it wasn't, grasp it with the tip of needle-nosed pliers and pull it out. If the adapter was glued in, heat it a little first, then remove it with needle-nosed pliers. Be careful to keep from grabbing the arrow shaft.

Installing the New Nock – Insert a new adapter into the arrow shaft if it is not already there or was damaged. Heat the adapter with a heat source and lightly smear it with hot-melt glue, then insert it in the arrow shaft. Allow it to cool.

Once the adapter is cool, push the nock into place, making sure the insert is completely inside the arrow shaft and there is no gap between the adapter and the base of the nock. Rotating the nock while inserting it often helps insure a tight fit. Align the nock with the fletching, making it match the other arrows in the set if this is a replacement.

Nocks that Fit Over the End of the Arrow Shaft

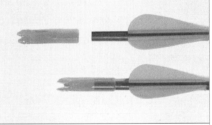

This style nock is used on carbon arrows. It protects the cut end of the arrow shaft. Like nocks inserted directly into the arrow shaft, these do not require glue.

Removing the Damaged Nock – Simply pull the damaged nock straight off the arrow shaft. Depending on the fit, this may be easy or it may take some effort. If you can't remove it with your fingers, use pliers, but be absolutely sure you are only holding the solid part of the nock with the pliers (not the part that goes over the arrow shaft). Pliers can crush the end of the arrow shaft, making it unusable.

Nocks that fit over the end of the shaft. These are almost always carbon arrows

Installing the New Nock – Push the new nock onto the end of the arrow. Again, this may be easy, or it may take some effort. The new nock *should* fit snugly but allow you to rotate it for alignment with the fletching.

One caution. Tolerances for nock fit are extremely precise. The diameter of some carbon arrows may not be as precise, so there can be some variation in how the nock fits on an arrow – anywhere from almost not being able to get the nock on the shaft to the nock falling off.

There's not a lot you can do if the fit is too tight, but if the nock is too loose you can increase the diameter of the shaft to hold the nock better. One solution is to apply a thin layer of glue – not to glue the nock to the shaft – but instead, to increase the diameter of the shaft slightly so the nock fits better. This requires a liquid or soft gel type glue, not hot-melt.

Put a *small* drop of glue on your finger and apply it around the end of the shaft where the nock will be, making a thin, smooth layer. *Allow the glue to completely dry (at least 15 minutes, preferably longer) so it will not adhere to the nock.* Then put the nock on the arrow and align it to the fletching. If the nock was quite loose, it may be necessary to apply another layer to build the diameter of the arrow. Just be sure the glue is completely dry before installing the nock. (If you glue the nock on the shaft, you may never get it off!)

Nocks that Use a Pin

These nocks go on high-end carbon/aluminum arrows, which are narrow. The pin inserts into both the shaft and the nock. If a nock is damaged, the pin could be also. Always check the pin when replacing the nock.

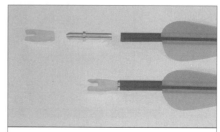

Nocks that use a pin to hold the nock on the arrow shaft.

The pins should be lightly glued into the arrow shaft, so when either initially installing pins or replacing a pin, low-temperature hot melt glue, pliers and a heat source (torch, etc.) are necessary. The nock is not glued.

Removing the Damaged Nock – Since these are not glued, they can be pulled off. If the fit is precise, it may take a little effort, even pliers.

Evaluate the pin. If there is any damage to the pin (ding, dent, or occasionally bent), it should be replaced. To remove the pin, warm the pin (*only the pin*) with the heat source, grasp the pin with pliers, and pull it out. *Never heat the carbon arrow.*

Before replacing the pin, evaluate the end of the arrow under good light. Occasionally the arrow was hit hard enough to crack the carbon on the end of the arrow, so look for that kind of damage. If the carbon is damaged, the arrow is not shootable.

Installing the New Nock – If you need to replace only the nock, push it onto the end of the pin and align the nock to the fletching.

To replace the pin, hold the new pin with pliers and heat the long end. When it is warm, rub just a little low-temperature hot-melt glue on it, pass it through the flame once more, and insert it into the end of the arrow. Allow it to cool, then replace the nock and align it.

Nocks that Fit on a Cone

These nocks are glued onto the cone (technically, a swedge) at the end of the arrow shaft.

You will need the appropriate glue (from an archery shop) to install these nocks. If you are replacing a nock you'll also need a moderately dull knife to remove the old nock (or what remains of it) from the shaft.

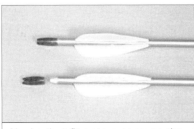

Nocks that fit onto a cone on the end of the shaft.

Removing the Damaged Nock – Work around the base of the nock, gently cutting the nock away from it. Make sure to cut only the nock material and not the aluminum cone underneath. Once the nock pops off, gently scrape any remaining glue off the cone.

Installing the New Nock – Put a *small* drop of glue either on the cone area of the arrow shaft or inside the hollow of the nock. Place the nock on the cone and with a slight pressure, rotate it to smear the glue around the cone. Then align the nock to the fletching and allow it to dry for 15 minutes or so.

Note: If you buy new arrows that are 'ready to shoot' and have this type of nock, check the nocks before shooting. Many shops just stick the nock on the arrow *without glue* for fletching. As discussed earlier, release and finger shooters require different nock alignment, so the shop lets you glue them and set the correct alignment.

Chapter 2
Fletching Arrows

The fletching stabilizes the arrow in flight and keeps the arrow flying smoothly. There are two main types of fletching. The type of fletching determines how you fletch the arrows.

- Fletching attached with glue
- Fletching attached with tape

Straight vanes and feathers are almost always fletched with glue.

Fletching is a detailed process with a number of decision points along the way. This Chapter presents information important to know and consider before fletching, as well as how to prepare for fletching. The specific procedures follow these discussions.

There are also discussions of the fletching jig and points common to both types of fletch- ing, including preparing the arrows. There is also information to help select fletching.

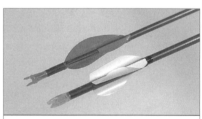

Curled vane and straight mylar vanes are fletched with tape.

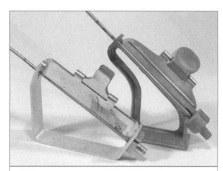

Different types of fletching jigs. These fletch a single arrow; there are others that hold up to 6 arrows or fletch three feathers/vanes at once.

The Fletching Jig

To fletch arrows, a jig is needed. There are many different styles of jigs in a wide price range. Better quality jigs are generally more adjustable and easier to set up for a specific arrow size.

There are two groups of jigs: those that hold a single fletching and those that allow you to apply all three fletchings at one time. Jigs that flectch a single vane or feather are generally more adjustable.

Parts of a Fletching Jig

Regardless of the brand, all jigs have some common parts. Find these on yours.

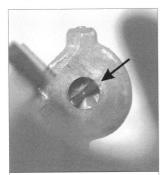

The nock sits over the receiver within the jig. This is the dark bar within the hole.

Receiver – This is a bar over which the nock sits. It keeps the arrow in position during fletching. Regardless of the brand, all jigs have a receiver. When repairing 3-fletch arrows, which way the nock sits on the receiver is important.

Holder – Almost all jigs that fletch a single vane or feather have a holder in which the arrow lies. The circular design of three-fletch jigs keeps the arrow in place, so they don't have this piece.

The arrow sits in the holder during fletching.

Dial – This allows you to turn the arrow in a single-fletch jig to apply the next fletching. It should be on the end of the receiver.

Clamp – A clamp holds the fletching while the glue sets. There may be one or three, depending on the design of the jig.

Types of Clamps – With most jigs, you have a choice of a straight or helical clamp. The clamp depends on the type of fletchng you use, which is influenced by your shooting style and the type of arrows. Information for choosing fletching is discussed under 'Choose the Fletching.'

Straight and helical clamps. The helical clamp puts a mild S curve curve in the fletching.

The dial on the end of the receiver rotates the arrow in the jig. The flat surface is aligned with the receiver.

Putting the Fletching into the Clamp – When putting the fletching into the clamp, allow the fletching to extend beyond the edges. This provides flexibility when pressing it onto the arrow shaft. If the fletching is too deep, it may be too rigid to seat firmly against the shaft; too far out, it may get distorted.

Leave a little space between the spine and the clamp.

Some experimentation may be necessary to determine how far out to place the fletching. For a starting point, allow approximately 1/8".

Putting the Clamp in the Jig – Some jigs that fletch a single vane or feather use a magnet to hold the clamp in place during flectching. Those without magnets have slots.

With either, a little practice is good so you don't get surprised when you start fletching. Some magnets are quite strong and jerk the clamp as you approach it. So for practice, put an unfletched arrow in the jig and position the clamp as you would if it held a feather or vane.

Placing the clamp on the magnet. Contact the magnet first. Also, touch the end of the clamp to the receiver to give a consistent spacing between the nock and the fletching.

Set the clamp against the magnets above the arrow shaft. Make sure the back end of the clamp contacts the jig near the receiver so the distance of the nock to the back end of the fletching is consistent.

If you were fletching, you would then gently press both ends of the clamp so the fletching would contact the arrow shaft.

On jigs without magnets, slide the clamp in the slots and make sure the entire length of the clamp contacts the arrow.

On three-fletch jigs, since the jig is round, some people put a rubber band around the clamps to keep them in place while the glue sets. If you want to use a rubber band, keep the pressure light.

Removing the Clamp from the Jig – To remove the clamp from the magnets, carefully *open it first* and then slide it away from the fletching, keeping it in contact with the magnets. Otherwise, you'll pull the fletching off as you move the clamp.

On jigs without magnets, make sure the clamp is open before removing it from the slot.

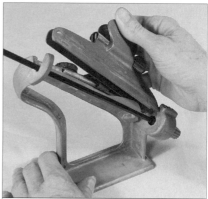
Open clamp before removing it from the jig.

Here are some guidelines when either setting up new arrows or when there is a need to change fletching.

Choosing New Fletching – There are a myriad of different fletchings on the market. With new arrows or refletching a whole set, you have free choice, but what you use partly depends on the kind of shooting you do and whether the arrows will be shot indoors, outdoors, on a target range, or on a field range.

For indoor shooting, many archers use a relatively large feather on a large-diameter, heavy arrow shaft. Weather is not a consideration, and feathers tend to be more forgiving.

For field shooting, there is more latitude in the type and size of fletching because most of the time the arrow is protected from wind. But rain is still a consideration. In general, vanes may be a better choice, but feathers are acceptable. The size is not as critical, so a larger vane is acceptable.

In contrast, for long-distance target shooting on an open field, small vanes are definitely better because 1) they retain their shape in the rain and 2) they are more accurate in the wind because the vane surface is smooth.

If you don't want to change fletching from indoors to outdoors, vanes are probably better. Many times it's what works best.

With a large, heavy arrow as is often used in hunting, it may be better to use a larger fletching because it provides additional stability. With large-diameter but very light target arrows, the fletching can be any size, but the extremes are probably not as good. Small, light target arrows usually work better with a small vane (either indoors or outdoors) or small to medium feathers (indoors).

There is also a lot of choice in the shape of the vane or feather. Shield cut, parabolic cut, rounded; high profile, low profile. If you are new to archery, probably the extremes are not as good. High profile vanes have a higher probability of striking the bow; low profile may not give as much stability as you need. The cut is not as significant unless you are an experienced archer and want to experiment.

Choosing Fletching for Repairs – When repairing arrows that are part of a set, keep one thing in mind – they need to be identical to what is on the other arrows.

Note: If only one feather or vane is damaged, it is still recommended to replace all the fletchings on the arrow. It is virtually impossible to refletch only one vane/feather *unless this jig was used for the original fletching and the nock has not been replaced or realigned on the arrow shaft.*

Vanes – Purchase the same brand, color, and size vane. Brands differ in length, height, stiffness, and color. Using a different size vane on some arrows may cause them to fly differently and group inconsistently. Even a different color of the same brand may be a little stiffer or softer, which can affect the shot pattern for precision shooters.

Feathers – These need to be the same length and come from the same wing of the bird (right wing or left wing). The wing determines which direction the barbs coming from the quill bend.

Right and left wing feathers. The barbs of the feather naturally curve; the direction of the curve is determined by which wing the feather is from. (Couresty National Archery Association)

Most commercial feathers are left wing, but check to be sure. Right wing feathers can be purchased, but they are usually harder to get. The color should match the rest of the set.

Set Up the Fletching Jig

The jig must be set so the fletching is properly positioned on the shaft. There are several steps to this.

Choose the Clamp – When repairing arrows in a set, the clamp must match what was used for the initial fletching. With new arrows, you can choose the clamp, but keep some thoughts in mind about the differences in clamps and what they do to the fletching.

Indoors, a lot of spin is desirable for stability, so many people fletch large feathers or vanes with a helical clamp. For outdoor shooting, most people use a straight clamp and offset the fletching on the shaft just a little to get maximum speed.

Very narrow high-end outdoor arrows have virtually no way to set an offset. In this case, a helical clamp set straight on the shaft gives the desired spin.

Straight Clamp – These keep the fletching perfectly straight. When using a straight clamp, you *must* offset the fletching for feathers and straight vanes, as previously discussed. Also, this is the clamp used for drawing the reference line for vanes requiring tape.

Helical Clamp – This clamp puts a mild S curve in the fletching, so an offset is not necessary. The curve makes the arrow spin in flight. The front and back ends of the fletching can be straight on the arrow shaft, which makes it work better on very thin arrows.

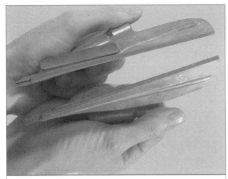

Left and right helical clamps. The curves go in opposite directions. This is important when fletching with feathers.

Helical clamps are left and right handed, setting the S curve in opposite directions (an S and a mirror S), setting the arrow to spin in opposite directions.

For vanes, using a left or right helical clamp depends on whether you shoot right or left handed. With a good setup it's not generally critical, but right helical usually gives more clearance for right-hand archers, while left helical works better with left-handers. So choose the clamp accordingly.

Clearance becomes important to a finger shooter when there is a bad release or the arrows are significantly too weak or too stiff for the bow. All of those make the arrow fly closer to the riser as the fletching passes the rest and button. The extra clearance the difference in rotation gives can make the difference between the arrow flying well or not (and therefore where it hits!).

Note: The direction of the helical clamp is critical when fletching feathers. It *must* be the same as the wing from which the feather was taken – right wing with a right helical clamp and a left helical clamp for a left wing feather. Otherwise, the clamp removes the natural curve of the feather barbs.

Set the distance from the Nock Throat – For finger shooters, the fletching should be as far back on the arrow as possible, but it must be enough forward of the nock to provide sufficient clearance for your fingers. Otherwise, your fingernail may tick the back edge of the fletching during release, creating erratic flight.

Keep the back edge of the fletching at least an inch forward from the throat of the nock. Long or large, meaty fingers may need a little more space.

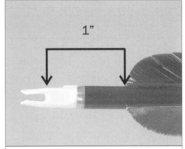

Distance from the throat of the nock to the back edge of the fletching should not be less than 1".

With a release, this is less of an issue, so the fletching can be positioned as you like. Many compound shooters put a high profile fletching a little more forward, but not more than 1 1/2" from the throat of the nock. Lower profile fletching is generally farther back.

How far the fletching sits from the back end of the clamp sets the distance between the nock throat and the back edge of the fletching (assuming the back edge of the clamp contacts the jig when fletching). Most clamps have a series of marks on the back end so you can set the fletching consistently from arrow to arrow.

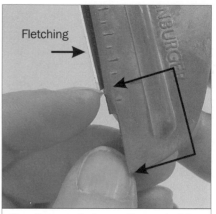

Determine how far forward you want the fletching. Put a mark on the arrow shaft where the back end of the fletching will be. Set it in the jig and determine which mark on the clamp is correct. Then mark the clamp for future reference.

The distance between the end of the fletching and the end of the clamp sets how far the back end of the fletching is from the nock. Use the same mark for all fletchings.

Center the Clamp on the Shaft – The fletching should be centered on the shaft, regardless of the diameter of the arrow. This is the left-right position of the clamp as the jig holds it. Centering the clamp puts it on the highest part of the curve of the arrow. Since each arrow size is different, the jig must be set for the size arrow you'll be fletching.

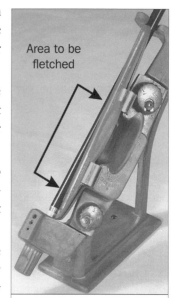

There should be a way to adjust the jig to move the clamp left-right on the arrow shaft. The exact method varies from jig to jig, so look carefully for how yours is adjusted.

Set the Offset – Arrows need to spin in flight to keep them stable as they travel to the target. Without spinning, the back end of the arrow can float or drift, creating inconsistent patterns.

The fletching makes the arrow spin. As long as the surface of the feather or vane is positioned any way except straight along the arrow shaft, airflow past it makes it spin. The more it spins, the more stable it is, but the quicker it slows down.

Straight clamp offset and centered on the shaft. This is a left offset. Also, the fletching will be towards the back of the clamp, so the top of the clamp looks farther off than necessary.

Arrow speed is important for outdoor target shooting, so generally the arrows are fletched to have less spin. Speed is not as important indoors because there is no wind and the distance is short, so lots of spin may be desirable.

Getting the arrow to spin is done one of two ways – by setting the vane or feather at an angle to the shaft or using a helical clamp. Both allow the vane to present a surface to the airflow. How much the arrow spins depends on the angle of the fletching in relation to the arrow shaft. This is important when using a straight clamp.

Note: The term to describe the angle of fletching relation to the arrow shaft is *offset*.

The Amount of Offset – What angle the clamp is set in relation to the arrow shaft depends on the shooting conditions and the arrow size. For background, read the discussion under 'Choosing New Fletching.'

Outdoor arrows need less offset; but always keep a little unless you are fletching curled vanes. Those can go on straight because the shape of the vane creates the offset. Indoor arrows can have as much as the arrow shaft will allow. The smaller diameter arrows (outdoor target arrows and arrows for youth) may limit how much offset is possible; there simply may not be enough width to put more than a tiny offset. Any more makes the ends of the fletching stick off the shaft. In this situation, a helical clamp and no offset may work better.

Right offset fletcing. The fletching sits diagonally to the right across the shaft.

The ***Direction of Offset*** – This sets which way the end of the fletching nearer the point sits in relation to the back end. For example, right offset means the front end of the feather/vane is to the right of the back end.

As with the left and right helical clamps, the direction of the offset makes the arrow spin either clockwise or counter-clockwise. As a general rule, the direction is not critical unless there is a problem with the fletching clearing the bow, but it is important for all arrows to have the same offset, so they all spin in the same direction.

When fletching vanes, the direction of the offset is usually determined by whether you are a right- or left-handed archer. Right hand – right offset; left hand – left offset.

With feathers, the offset *must* match the wing of the feather. As mentioned before, there is a natural curve to the feather barbs. It's necessary to keep that curve, so set the offset to match the wing – left offset for left wing feathers, right offset for right wing feathers. Setting the opposite offset removes that natural curve, making the feather stick straight up.

If you have clearance problems, the opposite offset may be better because it reverses the rotation of the arrow after it leaves the string. With feathers, reversing the offset requires feathers from the opposite wing. In any case, try changing one arrow, and shooting it to see if it gives more clearance.

Using Solvents

Some procedures in the rest of this Chapter recommend solvents for cleaning the fletching and/or arrow shaft. There are some things to know about using acetone, MEK, or other solvents. First and foremost, handle them carefully.

1) Never use solvents near an open flame, lighted cigarette, or other heat source. Properly dispose of used solvents and wipes in a closed metal container.

2) Wear safety glasses and avoid skin contact by using Q-tips or a similar applicator. Work in a well-ventilated area away from other people, animals, and especially children. If you're sensitive to solvent vapors, wear an approved respirator. Keep the cap on the container except when you're using it.

3) Be sure to read and understand the handling and safety directions on the product container. When purchasing solvents, ask for a material safety data sheet (MSDS). It explains the health and safety issues for that product. Suppliers are required by law to provide MSDS forms when requested.

Prepare the Arrows

Before fletching, the arrows need to be prepared. Whether refletching or setting up new arrows, the shafts must be clean and free of any residue.

Remove the Old Fletching

Fletching Attached with Glue – With a sharp knife or single-edge razor blade angled almost parallel to the shaft, carefully remove the fletching and as much of the glue from the shaft as possible. Be careful to not cut or gouge the shaft.

Scrape aluminum arrows firmly but gently. Small traces of residual glue can be removed using a solvent such as MEK or acetone.

Do not use solvents on carbon arrows. Instead, remove small traces of old glue by lightly rubbing the shaft with a very fine steel wool (such as grade 000). Use just enough pressure to maintain contact with the shaft, allowing the steel wool to slowly do the job. Using pressure on the steel wool could remove some of the carbon. When all traces of glue are gone, clean the shaft.

Fletching Attached with Tape – Pull off the vane and remove any tape around the arrow. Then work the tape adhesive off with your fingers. This can be tedious, but it must all come off before you can start with new tape. When it is free of any tape residue, clean the shaft.

Clean the Shafts

Clean both aluminum and carbon shafts with a low-abrasive cleanser, then rinse thoroughly with water and dry. *Do not* clean the arrow shaft with solvents such as acetone, alcohol, or MEK. Besides potentially damaging carbon arrows, they leave residual materials on any shaft.

Once you have the jig set and the arrows prepared, you can begin to fletch. Go to the discussion of the type of fletching you have. Each discussion provides the specific information needed for that type of fletching. They are in the following order.
- Fletching Attached with Glue
- Fletching Attached with Tape (There are two procedures, one for vanes and one for feathers.)

Fletching Attached with Glue

Both feathers and plastic vanes can be attached with glue. Vanes used with glue are almost always the straight, flat type with a spine that sits against the arrow shaft. The quill of a feather is the same as the spine of a vane.

The following materials are needed.
- Fletching
- Glue (see the next discussion)
- A fletching jig with the desired clamp, set up as previously discussed
- The fletching glue

The spine and quill on fletching.

The type of glue is determined by the type of fletching and the arrow shaft material. It is important to use the correct adhesive for a given fletching and arrow shaft combination; otherwise, the fletching may not hold well.

There are two basic types of glue. Most archery shops stock both.

Solvent Base Glue – This glue works well on fiberglass, wood, and aluminum arrows being fletched with either feathers or plastic vanes. It is the recommended type of glue to use with feathers.

Its advantage is the strong, pliable bond. The glue bonds well to both the arrow shaft and the vane/feather without excess penetration. The major drawback is the relatively long drying time, meaning the vane/feather must stay in the jig longer, and once removed, it is usually several hours before it is ready to shoot. Having several fletching jigs makes fletching quicker.

Most of these glues cannot be used on carbon arrows. However, a special formula is available for fletching vanes onto carbon arrows; be sure to read the manufacturer's recommendations before using it.

Solvent base glues typically contain methyl ethyl ketone (MEK). They should be handled with care; read the discussion under 'Using Solvents.'

Cyanoacrylate Adhesives (CA) – This glue works well for attaching plastic vanes to both carbon and aluminum arrow shafts. It is not recommended for feathers. This is a whole family of glues commonly available in hobby and craft stores as well as archery shops.

CA adhesives provide a strong but brittle bond that penetrates deeply into porous material. The deep penetration and the brittleness of the bond stiffens the quill of a feather, which is why they don't work well with feathers.

The big advantage is they are very fast setting – you can fletch an arrow in just a few minutes. One negative is most of these glues purchased at retail stores are very runny, making it difficult to use properly. The CA glue sold in archery shops is gel, which is much easier to use.

And handle the glue carefully – if you get it on your fingers, CA adhesives quickly stick them together! It's a good idea to purchase bond dissolving fluid when working with CA adhesives. This should be available where you purchased your glue.

One final comment about CA adhesives – they don't like moisture. If the glue gets very cloudy and white as it cures, there could be moisture on the arrow shaft. Fletching in high humidity also can make the adhesive become cloudy. This does not affect adhesion or durability; only it's appearance. But it sure doesn't look good!

Fletching the Arrows with Glue

To start fletching, you must have the jig set up and the arrows prepared. This procedure assumes these have been done.

1. **Prepare the Fletching** – (This Step is for solvent base glues. CA glue doesn't require specific preparation.) For better adhesion, some glue manufacturers suggest wiping the base of the plastic vane with acetone to remove residual oils and the plasticizer used in plastic products. Use a Q-Tip and swipe the base of each vane.

2. **Put the Arrow in the Jig** – Place the nock in the receiver and lay the arrow in the holder.

3. **Position the Fletching in the Clamp** – Follow the guidelines discussed earlier in this Chapter, setting the back end of the fletching on the mark and leaving the spine/quill a little off the edges of the clamp.

4. **Apply the Glue to the Fletching** – The key to good fletching with glue lies in how much glue you use and how well the vane seats on the shaft.

For **plastic vanes**, apply a *very* thin bead of glue down the center of the base. There should be only enough to cover the base of the fletching when it is pressed onto the shaft; no more.

Applying glue to a fletching. Sliding a finger along the clamp as you move helps keep the tube steady.

Note: The size of the hole in the applicator tip determines how much glue comes through, and therefore, the amount of glue applied to the fletch. With CA adhesives, in particular, this needs to be as small as possible.

Too much glue makes the excess squeeze out the sides and may keep the vane from properly seating on the shaft. With CA glue, the more glue, the longer it takes to cure. Too little glue means there is not enough adhesive to fully cover the base, leaving gaps that cause poor adhesion. If you're new to fletching, experiment to determine the right amount of glue.

Use only a thin bead of glue on a vane.

Feathers require a bit more glue than plastic vanes because the base of a feather is usually wider and more absorbent than the plastic. But again, the glue should only cover the surface of the quill.

5. **Place the Clamp in the Jig** – Carefully place the clamp so the edge of the fletching contacts the arrow shaft. (See the discussion in 'The Fletching Jig.') If you look closely at the base of the plastic vane as you press it, you can usually see the glue spread between the spine/quill and the shaft.

Apply enough pressure to spread the glue underneath the vane/feather and fully seat it, but be careful to keep from distorting its shape. This will take some experimentation.

Fletching properly seated on shaft. The edge of the clamp is parallel to the arrow shaft and the back end touches the receiver.

If you're using a jig that fletches three at one time, repeat Steps 3-5. Then use something to gently hold the clamps in place.

6. **Let the Glue Set** – With CA glue, let the assembly sit for 10 seconds or so. For solvent-based glues, this initial set time may vary, so be sure to read, understand, and follow the manufacturer's recommendations. Generally, it's between 15 and 20 minutes.

7. **Remove the Clamp** – Once the glue has set, carefully remove the clamp(s) from the jig as described under 'Parts of the Fletching Jig.'.

8. **Glue the Next Fletching** – If you're using a jig that fletches one vane/feather at at time, rotate the dial in the direction that keeps the fletching from touching the jig. Repeat Steps 3-7 to apply the remaining fletching(s).

   Note: Be careful – do not touch a newly-applied vane or have it contact anything. Until the glue is completely dry, bumping the fletching can knock it out of place. Initially it has only set enough to hold the fletching on the shaft.

9. **Spot the Ends** – When all three fletchings are on the shaft, *carefully* remove the arrow from the jig. Finish the job by applying a tiny drop of glue to both ends of the fletching as extra protection.

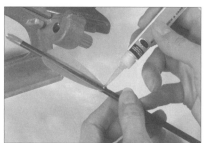

Set the arrow aside where the fletching does not touch *anything* and allow it to completely dry. CA glue will cure in a few minutes and can be used in as little

Put a drop of glue on both ends of each fletching to protect it.

as an hour. At a minimum, solvent base glue takes several hours to completely dry.

Fletching Arrows with Tape

Tape is generally used for mylar vanes, whether curled or straight. It is also possible to fletch feathers using a special tape. These are the two parts of this discussion.
- Vanes Attached with Tape
- Feathers Attached with Tape

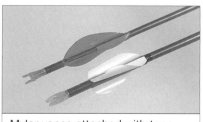

Mylar vanes attached with tape.

The tape used for fletching is a strong, thin, double-sided adhesive laid on the shaft. The fletching is attached to this adhesive. The tape supplied with the vanes is protected by a liner on each side.

The biggest advantage to using tape is once the line used to position the tape is marked on the arrow shaft, fletching is quick, easy, and can be done accurately without a jig. Also, since there is no glue, there's no glue odor.

Vanes Attached with Tape

Mylar vanes are strong, light and very thin. They come in a couple of shapes, the most common being the curled vane.

When fletching with tape, you need the following materials.
- A jig to mark the line on the arrow shaft. This can be either a standard fletching jig or the special tool designed for this. The tool is nice because you can easily carry one in your tackle box.
- A pencil or paint pen for a temporary or permanent tape line, respectively
- Q-tips
- Isopropanol (tape head cleaning fluid)
- The vanes
- The fletching tape that came with the vanes.
- Finishing tape that comes with some vanes. This is a single-sided tape used to protect the ends of the vane.

Note: If the vanes did not come with finishing tape, purchase either tape designed for model airplane trim at a hobby shop or auto pin stripe tape at an automotive supply store. Both are very thin, light, and strong, but the model airplane tape may be a little lighter. Both come in a wide variety of colors. Be sure to get self-adhesive trim material, not those requiring heat.

It is assumed the jig has been set up and the arrows prepared. If not, read the beginning of this Chapter for that information.

1. **Mark the Position of the Fletching** – Using a fletching jig or the special marking tool, mark three lines where the vanes will be positioned with a pencil or paint pen.

   For either, it is important to *indicate the exact position of the back end of the fletching on the shaft*. This must be the same for all three lines so all the fletchings are the same distance from the nock.

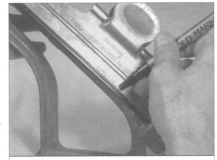

Mark three lines. Be sure to mark the position of the back end of the fletching.

If you are using a fletching jig, place the nock in the receiver and the arrow in the holder. Place the clamp against the shaft and draw a line. Rotate the shaft through the three positions, marking each one.

For the marking tool, follow the manufacturer's directions to place the arrow in it and mark along each of the three guides.

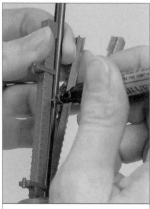

The marking tool can be used instead of the jig.

2. **Cut the Tape** – Tape that comes with the vanes can either be pre-cut or on a roll. If you must cut the tape, cut it *slightly* longer than the base of the vane.

Cut the strip of tape slightly longer than the vane.

Handle tape by the edges to avoid contaminating the adhesive surface with the natural oils on your fingers.

3. **Apply the Tape to the Shaft** – Remove the liner from one side of the tape and carefully position it along one line. Rub it gently to secure it.

Follow the vane manufacturer's guidelines about whether to put the tape on the right or left side of the line. For some vanes, this depends on whether the vane is left or right handed.

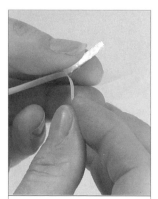

Remove the liner from one side of the tape. Note the tape is held only by the edges.

Apply the other pieces of tape to the shaft before attaching the vanes, making sure each piece of tape is on the same side of each line.

4. **Apply the Vane to the Tape** – Most manufacturers provide the specific procedures for applying vanes. The following is a discussion of the general procedure. It should work for most vanes.

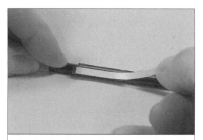

Apply the tape along one side of the line. Be sure the tape is on the same side of each line.

a. Hold the vane by the outside edge and lightly wipe the edge that will contact the tape with a Q-tip moistened with a *small* amount of Isopropanol. *Immediately dry the surface with a Q-tip,* as too much fluid will damage the surface of the vane. Allow the vane to dry before continuing.

Apply the vane to the tape making sure the back edge is on the positioning mark.

b. Once the vane is dry, remove the protective liner from the tape and carefully position the vane on the tape with the back end on the positioning mark. Rub the vane to anchor it.

c. Press the vane with a fingernail – hard – to speed adhering the vane to the adhesive and the adhesive to the shaft.

d. Repeat for the other two vanes.

5. **Finish the fletching** – Apply a single wrap of finishing tape around the shaft, covering the ends of the vanes. This holds the ends of the vane against the shaft. Do not use glue!

Pressing hard with a fingernail adheres the vane to the adhesive.

Apply the finishing tape.

Allow the tape to cure for 24 hours. In a pinch, you can use the arrow almost immediately, but it is better to allow the adhesive to fully bond with the vane and shaft.

Feathers Attached with Tape

This special tape made for feathers is stronger and a little thicker to provide a good contact with the quill. It is produced by only one manufacturer.

Fletching feathers with tape requires the following materials.

- A straight clamp. This keeps the feather straight. The quill has a strong natural curve, and itis next to impossible to keep it straight by hand.
- Either a standard fletching jig or the special marking tool for putting lines on arrows. (f you want to fletch feathers with a helical clamp, use glue.)
- A paint pen or pencil, depending whether you want a permanent or temporary line, respectively.
- The feathers

- Finishing tape. See the note after the materials list for 'Fletching Vanes with Tape.'

This procedure assumes the jig is set and the arrows are prepared. If not, read the information at the beginning of this Chapter.

1. **Mark the Lines on the Arrow** – Put three lines on the arrow shaft, following the procedure described in Step 1 for 'Fletching Vanes with Tape.' Make sure to indicate the location of the back end of the feather.

2. **Position the Feather in a Clamp** – Place the feather in the clamp, exactly where doesn't matter. Allow about 1/8" of feather to protrude along the edge.

3. **Apply the Tape to the Quill** – Cut a length of tape somewhat longer than the feather and apply it firmly to the quill. Trim the ends, leaving about 1/8" of tape beyond each end.

Apply the tape to the quill.

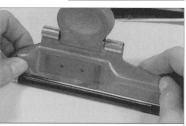

4. **Put the Feather on the Shaft** – Remove the tape liner, being careful to not touch the adhesive. Press the quill firmly in place on the arrow shaft along the line.

Run your fingernail down both sides of the quill to insure a good bond.

Place the feather on the shaft.

5. **Fletch the Other Feathers** – Remove the clamp and repeat Steps 2-4 for the other two feathers, making sure all three feathers are on the same side of the line.

6. **Finish the Fletching** – Place a single wrap of finishing tape around the shaft, covering each end of the fletching.

7. Allow the Tape to Set – Ideally, allow the adhesive to cure for 24 hours before shooting. In a pinch, you can probably use the arrows immediately.

Press the quill (and tape) against the shaft.

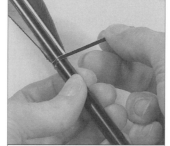

Apply the finishing tape.

Chapter 3
Cutting Arrows

Arrows are cut to fit the archer's draw length. To cut all arrows the same and protect the arrow from damage while cutting, a cutting tool is essential. Carbon arrows, especially, must be carefully cut to be sure the carbon stays undamaged.

Note: 1) Always use a cutting tool. Tube cutters and such devices crimp an aluminum arrow and can crush a carbon arrow. If the carbon in an arrow is damaged in any way, it is dangerous to shoot.

2) Before cutting arrows, check the cutting tool. The blade must be securely attached and completely intact and the motor must be properly aligned and securely mounted on the baseboard.

The Cutting Tool

An arrow cutting tool allows you to precisely set the length of the arrow. It also makes a clean, smooth cut.

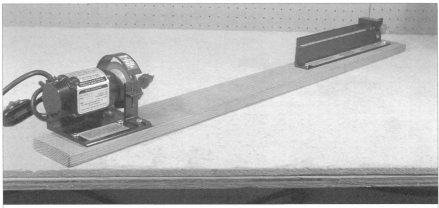

The arrow cutter. The motor rotates the cutting blade. On the other end, the arrow nock sits in the cup on the adjustment piece that slides to set the arrow length.

When setting the cutter for the desired arrow length, leave the motor off. This is just a measurement, so it is not necessary to have the blade rotating.

Note: 1) The arrows must have the nocks installed before cutting. This guarantees the length from the nock throat to the cut is precisely the same. See Chapter 1 for information on installing nocks.

2) While the cutter has a measuring guide, determining the arrow length by directly by working with the arrow guarantees proper arrow length.

When setting arrow length, the nock sits in the cup of the slide. The knob loosens the slide.

Set the Arrow Length – This must fit the archer. For experienced finger shooters, leave at least an inch of arrow in front of the button/pressure point. Arrows shorter than that often do not perform as well.

For youth and new shooters, the arrow should be even longer – as much as several inches beyond the bow, because the draw length may change as the archer becomes more proficient, and the extra length insures the arrow is safe.

When adding arrows to a set, the length must match the others. Remove the point from one arrow (see the next Chapter). Place the nock in the cup on the cutter slide, loosen the knob and move it until the cut end of the arrow shaft brushes the side of the cutting blade.

For arrows being added to a set, the end of an old arrow just brushes the cutting blade.

For new arrows, determine the length of the arrow shaft following the guidelines just discussed. Draw an uncut arrow and have someone mark where the cut is to be made. Or you have an arrow that is a good length from another set, use it as a guide. On the cutter, set the mark in line with the blade.

Setting the cutting tool for new arrows. The mark is in line with the cutting blade.

Cut the Arrows

Note: A couple cautions before beginning.

1) Cutting carbon arrows produces carbon dust, whether the arrow is completely carbon or carbon/aluminum. Either cut carbon arrows outdoors or run a vacuum, etc. while cutting to pull the carbon dust away as it is generated. Keep carbon dust from getting in the air where it could be inhaled by you,your family or your pets. Get rid of the dust once cutting is completed.

The end of a vacuum hose is clamped to the motor to remove carbon dust.

2) To protect your eyes, always use safety glasses.

1. Start the motor.

2. Place the nock in the nock cup.

Make sure the arrow nock sits in the nock cup before cutting.

3. Rotating the arrow smoothly on the cutting platform, lightly touch the arrow shaft to the cutting blade. Cut *around* the arrow, not across it. Use light pressure.

4. Continue rotating the arrow with a light touch until the extra length drops off.

5. Repeat this for each arrow.

6. When cutting is complete, turn off the motor.

Rotate the shaft to cut *around* the arrow, not across it.

Deburr the Arrows

Aluminum and aluminum/carbon arrows need to be deburred after cutting. Even using the lightest touch during cutting, there can be remnants of aluminum on the inside edge. These burrs need to be removed; otherwise, inserting a point can be difficult. A good cutter should have a deburring device.

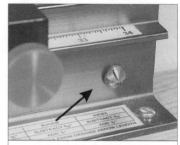

Deburring tool. Use with aluminum or aluminum/carbon arrows.

1. Place the cut end of the arrow against the deburring tool.

2. With a light touch, rotate the arrow shaft. Heavy pressure could spread the end of the arrow outward; not good.

3. Repeat for all arrows.

The arrows are now ready for the points.

Deburring the cut. Keep the touch light.

Chapter 4
Installing and Replacing Points

Points are necessary for any arrow. They must be installed on new arrows and replaced if they are damaged.

An arrow point has at least two parts – the *point* (what you see at the end of the arrow), and the *insert* that goes inside the arrow shaft. Some are a single piece, others allow you to remove the

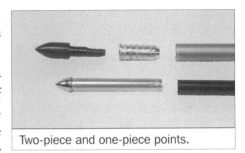

Two-piece and one-piece points.

point and replace it with a different weight point or a broadhead. Glue holds the insert against the inside of the arrow shaft.

Different arrows require different types of points, so if you are replacing some points in a set, purchase the same type. To be sure, remove a point and take it to the archery shop with you. Also, almost all target points have a selection of point weight, so be sure that is the same, too.

Whether you hunt or target shoot influences the type of point. Many hunters prefer a two-piece screw-in point so they can change from the standard target point to a broadhead without removing the insert. Target shooters almost always use a single-piece point.

Besides the points, some materials are needed to install or change points.
- A pair of pliers. Nock pliers work well because the round point fits into the round groove of the pliers, making it easier to hold. They can be purchased at most archery shops.
- A heat source (a propane torch, a burner on a gas range, even a cigarette lighter, although it's messy)
- A low-temperature hot-melt glue stick (from an archery shop)

When changing points, the old one must be removed. If you are building a new set of arrows, skip this part and just install the points.

Removing the Old Point

1. Gently heat the point with the heat source. If you hold the arrow an inch or so from the end of the shaft, you can feel the shaft warm as heat is conducted through the insert.

   With small diameter arrows (primarily carbon or carbon/aluminum), it is better to heat the point some, then wait 10-15 seconds to allow the heat time to conduct down the insert. Otherwise, there is a possibility of overheating the point, potentially damaging the carbon.

Heat only the point. Keep your finger near the end of the arrow shaft to feel when it is warm.

Important Note: Never heat a carbon arrow shaft directly. Anything above moderately warm can damage it. In general, whether carbon or aluminum, it is a good a practice to only heat the point.

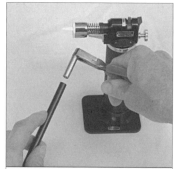

2. When you feel warmth through the shaft, grasp the point with the pliers and pull it out. Turning the point while pulling helps get it moving.

Removing the point.

Installing the New Point

1. Hold the *point* with the pliers and warm the *insert* with the heat source.

Heating the insert.

2. Pass the glue stick through the flame to warm it a little, then rub the insert, melting glue onto it. Rub glue completely around the end of the insert that goes deepest into the shaft. A lot of glue is not necessary.

Gluing the insert. Be sure there is glue completely around the end of the insert.

3. Insert the point into the shaft, rotating back and forth as you push the point so the glue smears around the inside of the shaft. When the insert is completely inside the shaft, there should only be a small ring of glue where the point contacts the shaft. Allow the arrow to cool.

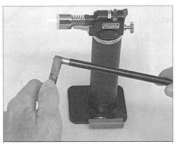

Inserting the point into the arrow shaft. Rotate the point as you push it into the shaft.

4. Once cool, the excess glue peels off easily. Trying to remove the excess glue too quickly will only smear it onto the arrow. If there is glue on the outside of the arrow, heat generated when the arrow hits the target may melt it and partially glue the arrow in the target, making it difficult to remove.

Peel off the ring of glue once it cools.

Keep Screw-In Points Tight

Keeping screw-in points tight (so they don't come loose and rattle) is a hassle for many archers. If you want to be sure they stay in place, warm the threads and lightly glue them. The point will not come loose, but it can easily be removed by heating.

Chapter 5
Checking Arrows

Arrow maintenance with nocks, points, and fletching is important. But equally important is making sure the arrow shafts stay in good condition. So periodically check the fletching, nocks and points. Along with those, check the arrow shaft with the procedures in this Chapter. There are two categories to check.

- Making sure an aluminum or aluminum/carbon arrow is straight
- Making sure there are no cracks or other damage to the carbon in carbon or aluminum/carbon arrows

Checking an Arrow for Straightness

Shooting a straight arrow is important for accuracy. (Shooting an arrow straight is also, but that's not covered in this book!) Arrows can bend from a number of causes. 1) In general, thin-walled aluminum arrows bend relatively easily. Large diameter aluminum arrows with a very thin wall (.012" wall, etc.) being shot out of a heavy draw weight compound have the potential to bend from the force of the shot – no other reason. 2) Arrows can bend if they are not pulled from the target in line with the line of entry. 3) If there is a miss from a bad shot, etc., and the arrow was wobbling in flight, whatever the arrow strikes as it passes can bend it.

Aluminum arrows can be straightened if there are no kinks in the shaft. Many shops have a straightener and will straighten arrows. Aluminum/carbon arrows are difficult to straighten, and if one is bent, generally it has to be discarded. Luckily, they don't bend easily.

There are two ways to check for straightness. The first, spinning the arrow against another arrow is easy and works well for almost any fletched arrow. To check the straightness of an unfletched arrow, you must spin it on your hand.

Spinning on Another Arrow or the Fingers

This spins the arrow by blowing on the fletching. While it works with any fletched arrow, curled vanes may not respond well.

1. With the point against the palm of one hand, lean the arrow either against an arrow held in the other hand or against two fingernails.

2. Blow moderately across the fletching to make it spin.

3. If the arrow is bent, you will hear and/or feel it wobble. Move the arrow/your fingers up and

Arrow sitting on another arrow.

Arrow sitting on fingers.

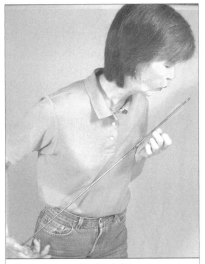

Blow across the fletching to make it spin.

down the shaft, checking for bends along its length.

Spinning on the Hand

This works for all arrows and is the only way to check an unfletched arrow. (Nothing is worse than tuning with a bent arrow!)

Initially this takes some practice, as timing and coordination must be developed. But once you get the knack, it's a quick and easy way to check arrows.

1. First check the point of the arrow. A chip or dent on the point will give a false reading, so replace a damaged point before continuing.

2. Hold the arrow between the thumb and first two fingers with the point on your palm.

3. With a quick motion of the fingers, flick the arrow to set it spinning. Keep it balanced on your palm as it spins.

Setting the fingers to start the spin.

A quick flick of the fingers makes it spin on the hand.

If the arrow is straight, the point will rotate smoothly on your hand. If there is any bend, you will feel a wobble. How severe the wobble is related directly to the severity of the bend. If the arrow is severely bent, you may not be able to spin it.

Checking a Carbon Arrow for Cracks

Carbon arrows periodically need to be checked for cracks or other damage to the carbon. Occasionally an arrow cracks for no apparent reason, and an arrow can get cracked if it hits something solid it passes on a miss. Shooting a damaged arrow is dangerous; it is particularly dangerous with completely carbon arrows, as they can shatter.

IMPORTANT: Handle a damaged carbon arrow carefully. The carbon in the damaged area is generally rough and often has splinters on the edges of the crack or break. If you accidentally get a splinter, make sure to remove all of it, *no matter how small*. It may be good to have a doctor check to be sure there are no fragments remaining.

Aluminum/Carbon Arrow Shafts – Under good light, look carefully for the following damage. Do not shoot an arrow with any of these.
• Cracks originating at either end of the shaft. These can be hairline and difficult to see.
• Gouging on anywhere on the shaft
• Compression on the shaft

Completely Carbon Arrow Shafts – Like aluminum/carbon arrows, these must have undamaged carbon to be safe to shoot. While cracks on the ends, compression, or gouging usually are visible, it can be difficult to see cracks in the shaft, so test them carefully.
• Check the ends for cracks
• Check for compression or gouging anywhere in the shaft.

You may not be able to see a crack in the middle of the arrow shaft. To check it, hold the shaft at both ends, bend, then rotate it. Any crunching or grating indicates damage.

Discard any damaged arrows.

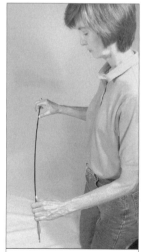

Checking a carbon arrow for cracks.

Part II: Working with Bow Strings

This section describes repairs, maintenance and other easy things you can do with bow strings, for whether compound, recurve, or traditional. In general, routine maintenance lengthens string life or makes it perform better with your arrows. The following items are discussed.

Chapter 6: Starting and Finishing a Serving – This is a general procedure used in other tasks described in the rest of this Part.

Chapter 7: Replacing a Center Serving – The center serving can easily be replaced, substantially increasing the life of the string.

Chapter 8: Adding a Loop to a Compound String – Some archers prefer this to either a loop on the release or hooking the string directly.

Chapter 9: Serving on a Nocking Point – This alternative to the clamped on metal nock set uses serving thread or dental floss.

Chapter 10: Making the Nocking Point fit the Nock – This increases the diameter of the string so it fits the nock.

Chapter 11: Installing a Peep Sight – Used by almost all compound shooters, proper installation keeps it aligned and in place.

Chapter 12: Installing a Kisser Button – Some archers like the additional reference point of the kisser button touching the lips.

Chapter 13: Waxing the String – Even though simple, there are some tips on how to most effectively wax the bow string to keep it protected from weather and wear.

Chapter 6
Starting and Finishing a Serving

This is a general procedure used in many of the procedures described in this section – replacing a serving and serving pieces into the string. Properly done, the finished serving is smooth and both ends of the serving thread are underneath the wraps of the serving.

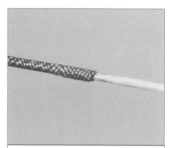

A properly finished serving. The wraps of the serving cover the end of the serving material.

Because it is not intuitive, getting comfortable with serving takes a little practice and requires a certain level of dexterity. It is a good idea to practice before trying it for real; take time, have patience, and work carefully. After a while this procedure will become second nature.

If possible, practice on an old string. Then no serious harm is done if you accidentally damage it. You should also practice removing the serving (which you may have to do sometime) without potentially damaging strand(s) in a good string.

Once you learn these two procedures, you will be able to do most of your own string maintenance. It also gives you more flexibility when you consider changing your equipment or when tuning.

Note: When these procedures are used in other Chapters, they are identified with Bold-Italics – *Starting a Serving* and *Finishing a Serving*.

Serving a string requires the following equipment.
- A spool of serving thread on a serving jig
- Scissors or a single-edge razor blade
- A pencil (not a pen!)
- A ruler or some measuring tool
- (Optional) A lighter or small butane torch

Before serving, mark the exact positon of the serving on the string. Center servings, peep sights, and kisser buttons must all be carefully positioned. *Use a pencil.* Some pen inks chemically interact with the string material, weakening it.

The Serving Jig – There are many types of serving jigs. All hold a spool of thread and have a way to insure the thread can be reeled off smoothly with the correct tension. If you can, try a few to see which you prefer.

Serving Thread – All serving material comes on spools similar to common thread used for sewing. Once you have selected the serving thread, the spool should be put in a serving jig and threaded as per the jig manufacturer's instructions. Serving materials are discussed in the next Chapter.

Different types of serving jigs. All hold the serving thread so it lays against the string during while serving and all have a way to adjust the tension of the serving thread.

The proper type and thickness of serving thread is important for a center serving; for peep sights and kisser buttons, it is not as critical.

Parts of the serving jig. The thread comes through the hole where it sits against the string. The wing nut adjusts the tension.

Starting a Serving

Starting a serving is relatively easy; the goal is to have the end of the serving thread under the wraps of the serving. The string needs to be under tension when serving, so string a recurve.

There are two ways to start a serving; the second is a variation of the first. Both methods work equally well, so use the one you like best.

1. Pull about a foot of serving thread from the jig and tighten the tension adjustment so the spool won't move in the jig.

2. With the jig hanging down, hold the end of the serving against the strands of the string *with the end pointing in the direction the serving will travel.*

3. Somewhere near the beginning mark, start hand wrapping, putting the wraps over the serving end, moving in the direction you want to serve. It doesn't have to be absolutely in the right location to start; just get the wraps over the end of the serving thread.

Make 4-6 wraps until the end is securely under the wraps.

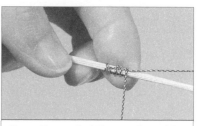

Cover the end of the serving with hand wraps. The end of the seving points to the right, the serving jig is hanging.

4. Pull both ends (the cut end and the end going to the spool on the jig) to tighten the wraps, putting enough tension on the wraps so it takes a little effort to move the serving into place. Otherwise, the end may come undone later.

5. Slide it to the reference mark for beginning the serving.

Tighten the wraps by pulling the ends. Once tight, slide it to the starting point.

6. Continue hand wrapping until there is a minimum of 1/2" of wraps to secure the end of the serving. Generally 5/8" to 3/4" is better. The wraps should be close together and reasonably tight.

Once you have hand wrapped the length desired, trim the cut end of the serving, then add a few wraps to cover it.

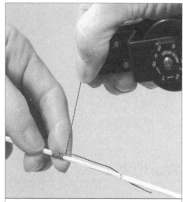

Continue hand wrapping for about 1/2" to secure the end of the serving.

7. Keeping tension on the end of the serving where it leaves the string, loosen the tension and turn the spool to take up the excess serving thread. This puts the jig against the string.

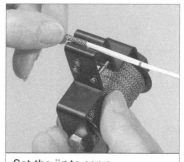

Set the jig to serve.

8. Begin wrapping, using the serving jig. Adjust the tension on the jig so the serving wraps tight but does not twist the string excessively as you continue adding wraps. With proper tension, the string wants to twist some; you'll have to hold it as you serve. But keep the tension loose enough so the serving jig moves around the string and doesn't just twist it.

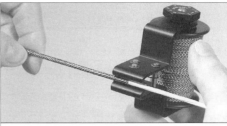

Serve with the jig. The tension needs to be tight enough to make the string want to turn a little as the jig moves around it.

The Variation

For some people, this is easier, and can be done on most recurve bows and lighter compounds. It may be difficult with strings on heavy draw weight bows without relaxing the bow, as the strands of strings on high draw weight bows may be difficult to separate.

1. Mark where the serving is to begin.

2. Near the starting mark, separate the strands of the string and insert the end of the serving thread through it. Try to get an equal number of strands on each side.

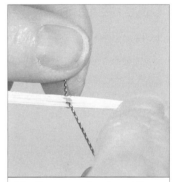

Starting a serving by putting the end through the string. It must be on the starting mark.

3. Move the serving thread to the mark. It needs to be there because once you start serving, it cannot be moved.

4. Lay the end against the string pointing in the direction the serving is to go.

5. Continue, starting with Step 3 in the previous discussion, making sure the wraps are tight and cover the end of the serving thread.

Begin the serving with hand wrapping. The wraps must be tight and close together.

Finishing a Serving

This completes the serving, making it look like the beginning – the end of the serving material is securely held under the wraps. No knots are used.

It is recommended to read through the procedure and study the illustrations to get a relatively good idea of what to do before attempting the serving. This is not necessarily intuitive, so some practice is recommended.

1. Mark the string at least 1/2" before where you want the serving to end. This determines the length of serving under the wraps.

2. Serve up to that point with the serving jig.

3. Note the direction you've been serving. Does the jig move over, down, and away from you, or is it coming up and over the string towards you? Keep this in mind throughout the rest of this discussion.

4. Hold the wraps against the string so they don't come loose. Pull out at least a foot of serving material from the jig. You may have to loosen the tension on the jig to do this, but once done, tighten the tension so the spool does not move in the jig. You will not be using the jig for serving from now on.

5. Keeping tension on the serving thread coming from the wraps (so they do not loosen), make a loop with the thread. One end is the end of the wraps already done, the other is the string material against the string several inches away.

   Which direction the loop goes is set by the direction you've served so far. It needs to be in the same direction. For example, if you're serving up the string, the end of the serving nearest the serving jig should be above the served area on the string.

   Also, *from now on, you must keep tension on the end of the serving coming from the wraps already on the string.* Otherwise, they will loosen.

Make a loop to finish the serving. The left hand keeps tension on the wraps. The jig will go through the loop, putting wraps on the string inside it.

6. Estimate the number of wraps needed to serve 1/2" or more by counting threads on the area already served. Then put the jig through the loop, adding that number of wraps inside it lightly and by hand. The jig moves arouond the string in the same direction as the wraps already there (determined in Step 2), *but the wraps are added to the string in the opposite direction.*

All the while, keep tension on the end coming from the wraps already served. It may take a little practice to develop the dexterity to keep tension so the wraps on the string stay in place while adding the new wraps. Initially it feels like you need 3 hands!

This is preliminary wrapping. It doesn't have to be pretty; just get the wraps around the string. *Keep the wraps from laying over one another.*

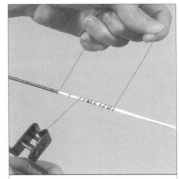

Add loose wraps inside the loop. Note the end mark on the string – in the finalhand wrapping, these must cover the string to that mark. The left hand keeps tension on the finished wraps through-out.

7. Once you have the needed number of wraps within the loop, (again maintaining tension on the wraps), loosen the tension adjustment of the jig and play out enough serving material to take the thread back past the end of the serving already done on the string. Retighten the tension adjustment.

8. Lay the serving over the end of the wraps and hold both in place with one or more fingers.

9. With the other hand, keep tension on the loop to keep it from moving, continue wrapping tightly alongside the wraps already there. (Yes, doing both can be a challenge!)

The preliminary wraps inside the loop will unwrap as you continue.

11. Hand wrap the remainder of the serving. When complete, there should be only a loop at the end of the serving. (Keep tension on it to keep it from twisting!)

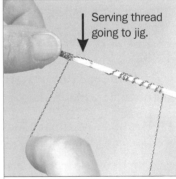

Serving thread going to jig.

Do the final hand wrapping. The thread from the serving jig is held in the left hand against the string.

12. Holding the loop with a finger, pull the serving thread from where it emerges from under the wraps. Reduce the loop to around half an inch. Keep tension on the loop while doing this, otherwise it *will* twist on itself.

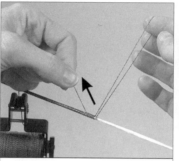

Completion of the hand wrapping leaves one large loop. Keep it under tension.

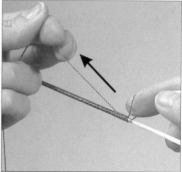

Pull the serving through. Keep the loop under tension.

If you pull the loop completely through without maintaining some tension on the loop, you'll have a little nub of twists on the end of the serving with no way to fix it.

13. Using the point of a pencil or some other pointed tool, pull the rest of the loop out. Done correctly, it will be a clean, smooth serving.

14. Cut the serving thread where it leaves the serving. Either leave about 1/16" protruding to melt the end (the next step), or cut it as close as possible without damaging the serving.

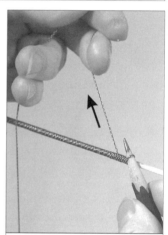

Finish pulling the serving through with a pointed object.

15. (Optional) A final touch is to *carefully* melt the end of the serving to produce a hard little ball right next to the serving. This locks the end of the serving in place, preventing it from being drawn back into the wraps, possibly coming loose later. This requires a lighter.

Wave the side of the flame past the protruding end of the serving quickly enough to keep from damaging the serving, but slow enough to melt the fibers on the cut end to form the ball. *Do not use the end of the flame.* It is too hot and will melt the serving.

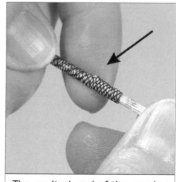

The melted end of the serving produces a tiny ball.

Chapter 7
Replacing a Center Serving

The serving in the center on a string protects it from wear from the fingers/release and from hitting/touching the arm-guard on the shot. So it wears more than the rest of the string and may need replacing even though the rest of the string is fine. This substantially increases the life of the string.

There are three points of consideration: the type of serving material, its color and the diameter of the thread. While color is decorative, the material and the thread diamter can be important for performance.

Choose a Serving Material

There are three things to consider when selecting serving material.

Material – Serving thread is made from a number of different materials. Monofilament and multi-filament nylon are the most common; both are quite durable. There are also newer synthetic servings, chemically similar to the string material, that are extremely tough. They are difficult to cut and will dull cutting edges (scissors, etc.) relatively quickly. And there are some blended serving materials that use natural fibers.

The most popular servings are braided: many strands braided together to form a strong thread, similar to a piece of string or rope. It is strong, durable, and easy to use. Multifilament braided material is never smooth.

Monofilament nylon serving is similar to fishing line or a strand of wire – a single strand of extruded synthetic fiber, with a hard, smooth surface. It is often found on commercially-made strings because it works better in a string-making machine and is fairly inexpensive. Some people think monofilament provides a smoother release for finger shooters. Others

The center serving on a recurve bow string.

complain it comes loose quicker. If you are undecided, try both and use the one you prefer.

Color– Serving comes in a wide variety of colors so you can accent your equipment or color-code your strings. But one caution – because of the difference in how the color is set in the serving, some colors rub off.

Most servings are pastel or light blue, light brown, beige, light green, etc., or black. The color is dyed into the serving, so the dye penetrates the thread fibers. Until recently, most bright colors – reds, yellows, and fluorescents – were made by embedding fine pieces of color in wax, then coating the serving thread. The wax rubs off on anything it contacts and colors everything the serving touches. New dyes can now produce the bright colors in the serving thread, so you can have vibrant colors in your servings without the problem of the wax.

Thread Diameter– Different serving threads are different diameters; some threads come in several diameters. The thread diameter is a factor in proper nock fit.

For example, a 14-strand string is considerably thinner than an 18-strand string, but the nock may be the same size or have the same throat size. Therefore, to have the nock fit properly on both, an 18-strand string requires a thinner serving thread, while the 14-strand string needs a thicker serving.

Braided serving is produced in a number of thicknesses, measured in thousandths of an inch. The common diameters are .018, .019, .021, .022 .024, and .025. This gives you flexibility in getting the nock to fit correctly.

Replacing the Serving

To replace a serving, you need the following materials.
- Serving thread on a serving jig.
- Bow Square
- Pencil
- Scissors or other cutting tool
- (Optional) A lighter (not a torch)

Note: This procedure builds on the information for *Starting a Serving* and *Finishing a Serving*, as described in Chapter 6. If you are not familiar with the serving process, be familiar with the procedures in that Chapter before attempting to replace any center serving.

1. *Determine the Position of the Serving on the String* – This depends on whether you want the serving to be in the same location or whether you want to reposition it. Once you determine where to place the serving, using a pencil, mark both ends.

Serving in the Same Place – If you are replacing a center serving, mark the top and bottom edges before removing it. If it has already been removed, look carefully at the string. On light-colored strings, the area under the serving usually is not as soiled; on either a dark or light string you may be able to see where the wraps of the serving ended. Use this as a guide for positioning the new serving, unless it was improperly placed initially. (That sometimes happens!)

If you can see where the old serving was, it's probably best to reserve the same area. That way, you don't change the weight of the string significantly (more important for recurve shooters) and therefore, if the serving material is the same as the original, it should perform similar to what it was before.

Repositioning the Serving – If the serving was not where it needed to be, mark the area to be served cover before beginning the serving process. The general rules are as follows.

For finger shooters (both compound and recurve) the serving must extend above where the fingers contact the string, but it does not need to be significantly more. The serving should extend below the nocking point far enough to protect the string from contact with the armguard or anything else it may rub against during a shot.

For release shooters, it is not necessary to have the serving as far above the nocking point on the string. At a minimum, make it long enough so the release, release rope or string loop is below the wraps cover the end of the serving. Unless you're looking for absolute ultimate performance, the usual amount of serving above the nocking point will not cause any difficulty or lack of arrow speed.

2. *Mark the String* – If you're serving the string for the first time, initially determine the point perpendicular to the rest and mark the string with a pencil. Then measure above and below the mark to set the length of the serving.

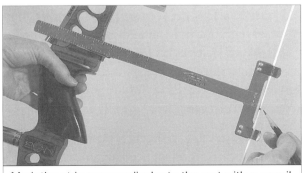

Mark the string perpendicular to the rest with a pencil.

As a general rule for finger shooters, if the serving covers 2" to 2.5" above the perpendicular to the arrow rest and 5" below perpendicular, it should protect the string well. If you have an unusual setup, adjust it, but make sure it covers all areas that

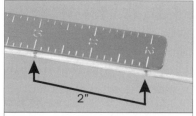

Make a mark two inches above for recurve shooters.

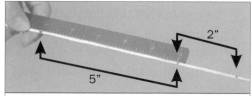

Add five inches below perpendicular for a total of seven inches. The end of the ruler is on the perpendicular mark.

may wear when shooting. For release shooters it's similar, but can have a little less serving above.

3. *Determine the Direction of the Wraps* – Finger shooters must take the direction the serving is wound into consideration. The string rotates in the same direction the fingers come off the string at the release and determines the direction of the serving. If the serving is wrapped the opposite direction, it will eventually come undone.

Looking down the string from the upper limb, the release of a right handed shooter makes the string rotate clockwise, while a left handed shooter

On release, the string rotates clockwise, so the serving should alxo be clockwise.

rotates the string counterclockwise. The wraps must go in the same direction as the rotation of the string – right for right handed and left for left handed.

The serving needs to be wrapped counter-clockwise for a left-hand shooter.

Therefore, using the upper mark (closer to the upper limb) for the starting point, the direction of serving for a right handed archer wraps under the string as it comes toward you (clockwise if viewed from the upper tip), moving from upper limb to the lower limb. For a left handed shooter, the serving wraps over the top of the string as it comes toward you (counterclockwise) while serving from upper to lower limb.

4. *Start a Serving* at the correct mark, moving in the direction necessary and wrapping around the string in the direction just determined.

5. **Serve the string.** As mentioned in Chapter 6, set the tension on the serving jig so it is tight enough to keep the serving in place. The string will want to turn some as you wrap, but not much that the string significantly turns with the jig as you move around it.

If the serving is loose, it can develop gaps within a relatively short period of time, requiring a replacement before it otherwise would be needed. If the serving is too tight, it tends to bind the strands of the string and can cause excess wear and premature string failure.

6. Continue to within 3/4" of the end mark and *Finish the Serving*.

Chapter 8
Adding a String Loop to a Compound String

Many compound shooters prefer the release to hold the string directly behind the vertical center of the nock. This evenly distributes the pressure of the string on the nock during the shot. If you prefer this, the release holds a loop on the string instead of holding the string.

Adding a string loop or replacing the existing loop is easy. The most common method of attaching this loop is a special knot that tightens with pressure.

You'll need the following materials.

- A length of release rope. If you are replacing a loop, it should be the same type as the present loop.
- Scissors
- A heat source, preferably a torch that burns clean

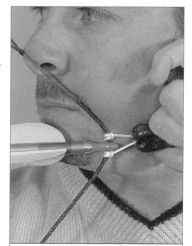

A string loop evenly distributes the pressure of the string on the nock during the shot.

The Length of the Release Rope – When replacing the string loop, remove the loop from the string and measure it. Then add 1/4" to allow for burning the ends. If you are modifying your anchor or draw length, adjust the length of the as needed. But always add the extra 1/4".

If you're adding a loop for the first time, it may be necessary to experiment a little to get the length right. At a minimum, make the string loop long enough for your release clasp to clear the back end of the nock. Then add 3/4" for each knot and the burning of the ends. The string loop can be as long as desired, but an overly long loop is not necessary.

This procedure ties two knots on the string, one above the nocking point, one below.

When starting, don't worry about precise positioning. Put it close to where the nocking point should be, and once completed and tested, set the nocking point. The knot can easily be loosened for adjustment.

1. Cut a length of the release cord to be used for the loop.

2. Using the end of a knife or other pointed piece, flare the end of the release rope to separate the strands. Then using the heat source, melt the end to create a bulge. Allow it to cool. Repeat for the other end.

   Flare, then melt both ends of the release rope.

   This bulge is important, as it keeps the knot from slipping. Don't make it too big, but be sure it bulges evenly around the rope.

   The melted end must have a small bulge to keep the finished knot from slipping.

3. Place the release rope around the string near the nocking point.

   Starting the knot.

5. Cross the ends of the rope over the string.

6. Take the end pointing back and bring it forward around the longer end of the rope.

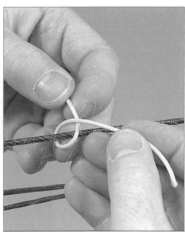

Cross the ends of the cord.

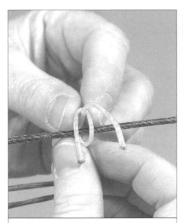

Bring one end around the other.

7. Take the same end around the string again. This creates a small loop around the longer end of the rope.

8. Stick the same end of the rope through the small loop just created. The end will lie next to the longer part of the rope.

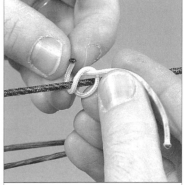

Take the same end around the string to form a loop.

9. Pull the long end of the rope tight to secure the knot. The bulge at the end of the rope should lie against the small loop around the string.

This finishes the knot on one end. Now do the other.

Pull the rope tight to secure the knot.

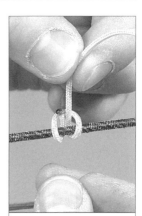

Put the end through the small loop. It lies alongside the other end.

10. Take the long end of the release rope and make a larger loop (the string loop when finished) to the other side of the nocking point. With the rope on the same side of the string, take the cord around the string, then through the string loop. Then bring the end around.

11. Going around the string again, stick the end through this second small loop.

12. Pull the cord on the release loop snug to secure the knot.

Beginning the second knot.

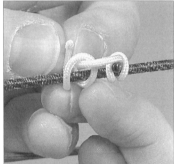

Take the end around the string and put the end through the small loop.

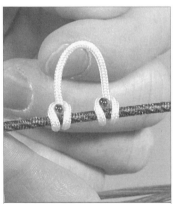

The completed release loop. Test it before shooting.

Before shooting, test it carefully to be sure both knots will hold the draw weight. With your release, draw the string a few inches, then let down. Check the knot. Do this several times, drawing farther and farther. At any point, if either bulge shows any sign of slipping through the small loop, either remove the loop, burn the ends more so the bulge is larger, and redo the knots, or use a new piece of rope, making the bulges larger.

When complete, set the nocking point. As stated before, the knots can be easily loosened to set or adjust the nocking point.

Chapter 9
Serving on a Nocking Point

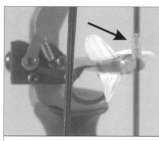

A nocking point served on with serving thread.

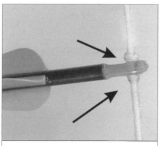

Two nocking points served on with dental floss.

No matter what style you shoot, the bow must have a fixed nocking point. Usually it is either served on or is a metal nock-set clamped onto the string. Because of the extra weight of the nock-set, some recurve shooters prefer to serve on a nocking point. And many compound shooters like the flexibility of adjusting a served on nocking point.

So there are two methods of serving on a nocking point; both work well. However, which one is best partly depends on the type of bow you shoot and whether the weight of the string is significant.

Method 1 – Using Serving Thread

This is used by many compound archers and a few recurve shooters. On a compound, it leaves a way to readjust the nocking point.

You need the following materials.
- A thin serving thread or heavy sewing thread. On a compound it's pretty much preference. Recurve shooters generally prefer to keep the string weight as light as possible, so the thinner the thread, the lighter the string will be.
- Scissors or a way to cut the thread
- A heat source, preferably a small torch

Note: The position of the nocking point is part of tuning and its location is not discussed here. But it should be set before doing either of these procedures.

1. Cut a length of serving thread 8-10" long.

2. At either the bottom or top edge of the nocking point (depending on whether you are serving the nocking point above or below the arrow), tie an overhand knot on the string. You will be working from the nocking point outward, away from it.

3. Bring the ends around to the other side of the string and tie another overhand knot opposite the one already done.

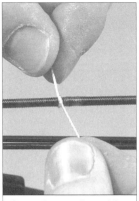

Start the serving with an overhand knot.

A second overhand knot on the opposite side.

4. Work away from the nocking point, tying overhand knots on opposite sides of the string. Do this 10-12 times until there is about 1/2" of serving material on the string.

5. Double knot the ends of the serving. Pull this knot relatively tight, as some serving materials start coming loose as soon as the tension is released.

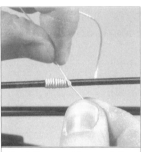

End the nocking point serving with two knots.

6. Cut the ends, leaving 1/8" of thread beyond the knot.

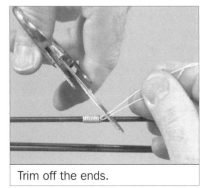

Trim off the ends.

6. With the *side* of the torch flame, lightly brush the ends of the serving thread with the side of the flame several times. This melts the serving thread, creating a small ball on the end of the serving thread. It insures the knot does not come undone.

Caution: Always use the side of the flame. This keeps the heat of the flame away from the string material and melts only the ends of the serving thread.

7. Repeat on the other side of the nocking point.

Lock the knot in place. With the side of the flame, brush the ends of the serving to create a melted ball next to the knot.

Method 2 – Using Dental Floss

A nocking point served with dental floss is an alternative to the metal nock set if you're looking to reduce the weight of a recurve string. It can make a significant difference in arrow tuning if you're trying to make the arrow perform weaker.

To make the nocking point most effective, keep it relatively small. A small nocking point will hold the arrow in position just as well as a large one. If it gets large, it can interfere with the tab/glove, and besides, if you're looking to reduce string weight, the extra material just adds weight back on.

A couple items are needed for serving on the nocking point.
• Dental floss/tape or thin, strong thread. (This can be waxed or unwaxed, although waxed is easier to use.)
• Scissors
• Fast-drying glue

First determine where the nocking point should be. That is part of tuning and is not addressed here. What is important is knowing where the *where to start if you are serving a nocking point above the arrow.* Put a mark at this point.

1. Cut an 8"-10" piece of dental floss.

2. Just outside the mark (in relation to where the arrow sits), tie a simple overhand knot around the string.

3. Take the ends around to the other side of the string and tie another overhand knot.

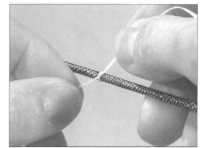

Start the nocking poing with an overhand knot.

4. Repeat this, keeping the knots on top of each other, creating a small bulge on the string.

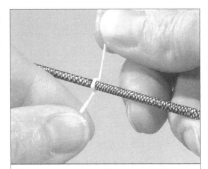

Second overhand knot; on the opposite side.

5. When you have about half the desired size of the nocking point (it doesn't take many knots), put a *small* drop of glue on the knots and spread it around. Not much is needed.

6. Add overhand knots on alternating sides of the string until you reach the desired size.

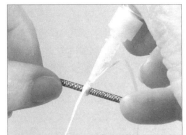

Add a drop of glue when the nocking point is about half the desired size.

7. Cut the ends off the remaining thread, leaving about 1/8".

8. Put another small drop of glue on the nocking point.

9. Press the ends down onto the surface of the nocking point in the direction they naturally want to lie. You may have to wait until the glue to becomes tacky enough to hold the ends down.

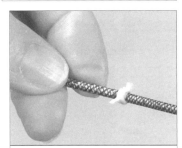

Once the nocking point is the desired size, trim the dental floss, leaving a little end on both.

Once the ends are glued down, allow the glue to thoroughly dry.

If desired, repeat on the other side of the nocking point.

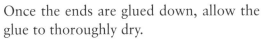

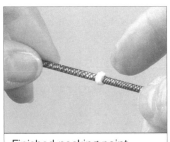

Finished nocking point.

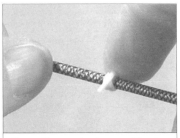

Press the ends down with glue.

Chapter 10
Making the Nocking Point Fit the Nock

A nock should stay on the string by itself without requiring it be held with your fingers. Nock fit on the string is important for consistent performance. The nock should neither fall off by itself or with just a touch, nor be so tight it takes effort to snap it on the string.

Note: Most nocks snap onto the string with a sound and feel of 'click.' A few, particularly on wooden arrows, do not click; they just slide. With either, the string must sit in deepest part of the nock throat.

If the nock throat is too large, you can increase the diameter of the string by either replacing the center serving with a thicker material or by adding a layer of dental floss to the nocking point. This Chapter describes how to add thickness with dental floss. See Chapter 7 for replacing a center serving.

The nocking point must be set, add one if necessary. Where it is located is part of tuning and is not discussed here.

The materials are needed can be purchased at any grocery or drug store, but generally it is better to get the glue from an archery shop.
• Quick-drying glue
• A 10" piece of dental floss or dental tape
• Scissors

Building the Thickness

Place the arrow on the nocking point to determine the width of the nock on the string, then remove it. Mark the location if necessary.

1. At the bottom of where the nock sits, lay one end of the dental floss on the string with the end pointing towards the lower limb.

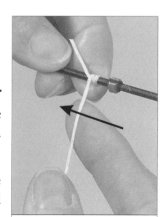

Start the serving. The initial direction is away from the nocking point.

2. Working downwards, wrap over this end, adding 3-4 wraps. Wrap clockwise (as seen from the upper limb) if you are right-handed; counterclockwise if you are left-handed).

3. Bend the end of the dental floss upward and do 2-3 wraps over it and over the layer just served. This wraps over the end of the dental floss anchors it so it will not come loose, and keeps the nock from sliding downward on the string from top finger pressure.

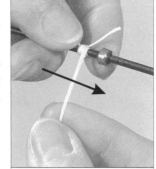

The return serving covers the folded end of the dental floss and the layer of serving already there.

4. On the area where the nock sits, continue wrapping the floss, spacing the wraps to build the correct thickness. Check it with an arrow; it should feel just a little tight. After a little shooting, it compresses.

This spacing controls the thickness. The closer together the wraps are, the thicker; the farther apart, the thinner. The wraps do not have to touch. You may have to try several times to get the correct thickness.

Dental tape is flat. You can make the tape lay flat against the string, making it easier to adjust the thickness by the spacing.

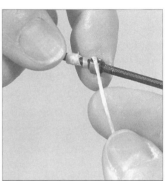

How close together the wraps are determines the thickness under the nock.

6. Finish by taking the dental floss above the nocking point and *Finish a Serving*, discussed in Chapter 6. This only needs to be 5-6 wraps, b ut they should be tight.

This extra layer of dental floss will wear with use and probably will have to be replaced periodically. It may help to put a thin layer of glue on the surface to help keep it in place.

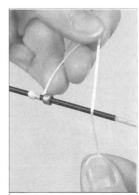

Finish the Serving above the nocking point.

Chapter 11
Installing a Peep Sight

Almost all compound archers and a few recurvers use a string peep. With it, you look through the string, eliminating the necessity of consciously maintaining string alignment at full draw. It also keeps the distance from the nock to the eye consistent, which helps when shooting long distances.

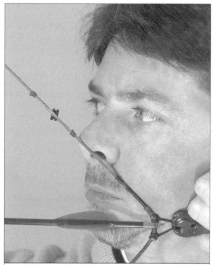

A string peep keeps the string in line with the line of sight. It is not legal for all shooting styles.

Note: In some competition divisions, a string peep is not allowed. If you are considering using one, check the rules for your type of bow and your division to be sure it is legal.

Peep sights are different for compound and recurve bows. Because the string angle is much more acute on a compound, the string slot on the side of most peeps are angled so the peep is vertical when the string is at full draw. Since the string angle is much less on a recurve, the string slot runs the length of the peep. When purchasing a peep, be sure you get one that suits your bow.

If your string already has a peep installed and you are replacing the string, measure the distance from some point on the nocking point to the peep before removing it from the string, Use this measurement to position the peep in the new string. See the last discussion in this Chapter.

To insert a peep, you need the following materials.
- The peep
- A bow press for a compound. Archery shops generally have a free-standing bow press. You can also purchase a portable press which is easily carried in your bow case or quiver.
- Serving thread

- Scissors
- A heat source, preferably a small hand-held torch
- A ruler to measure the position of the peep once installed

Install the Peep

Insert the Peep in the String

Note: The discussion that follows is for compound bows, because a peep is used more often with a compound.

1. Put the bow in a bow press and relax the bowstring.

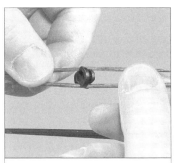

Peep inserted in the string. There are an equal number of strands on each side.

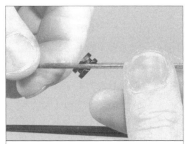

An angled peep works better with the severe string angle on a compound. The grooves on the side hold it in position.

2. Above the center serving, count the number of strands in the string and divide the string into two groups with an equal number of strands.

3. Insert the peep between the two groups of strands. Be sure all strands sit in the grooves on each side of the peep.

4. Remove the bow from the bow press.

Once the peep is in the string, position it horizontally and set it so you can see through it at full draw. This takes a little time and requires attention to detail. Otherwise, it may not be easy to use and could produce inconsistent groups.

Determine the Vertical Position of the Peep

The nocking point should be set before setting the peep. The distance between the arrow nock and the peep is critical, and any changes in nock location will require repositioning the peep. If you are replacing a string that has a peep in it, use the measurement you made before removing the string from the bow and go to 'Align the Hole in the Peep.'

1. Draw the bow back with an arrow, pointing at a target, just like you do when shooting. *Drawing a bow with an arrow should only be done at an archery range.* Close your eyes as you come to anchor.

2. Once at full draw, open your eyes. Vertically, is the peep in line with your line of sight? (It may be turned so you can't look through it; that's the next step.) If not, let down and slide the peep up or down the string. Repeat this until your line of sight is in line with the center of the peep.

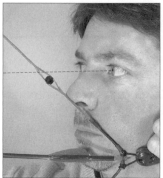

Peep out of position. It is too low and is turned 90° to the line of sight.

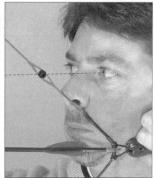

Peep in proper vertical position, but it is still turned.

Important – Keep your head still. An inconsistent head position gives an inconsistent reading. Closing your eyes helps this.

If the peep is turned so you can't see through it, get it as close as you can, get the hole aligned (at least pretty well), and check this again.

3. Mark the string at the center of the peep. This gives you a check to be sure the peep stays positioned when aligning and serving it in place.

Align the Hole in the Peep

This sets the peep so you can see through the hole at full draw. The hole must be straight in line with your eye and the scope lens. Otherwise, arrows will go left-right, especially if you use a peep with a lens.

The string may rotate a little as you draw, so don't use the resting position as a measure. It can only be judged at full draw. The difference in position is smaller with a release, and may be dramatically different with fingers.

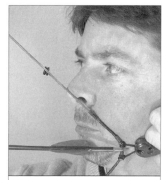

Peep properly aligned in the string. It is perpendicular to the line of sight.

If you've purchased a tubed peep, skip this. The peep will automatically align because of the tube.

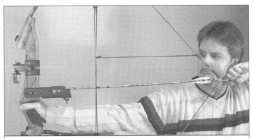

Tubed peep. Because the tube stretches with the draw, the peep is always aligned. Be sure attachment of the tube is solid.

Aligning the peep can be done one of two ways.

Method 1: Move Strands in the String – Moving strands from one side of the peep to the other turns the peep in relation to the bow, aligning it to your line of sight.

1. Put the bow in the bow press and relax the bow string.

2. Move strands from one side of the peep to the other, always keeping the same number of strands on each side. In other words, if you have an 18-strand string, keep 9 strands on each side of the peep. Move a couple strands from one side to the other, then take a couple strands from the second side and move them back to the first side.

3. Remove the bow from the bow press and check the alignment at full draw.

4. Repeat this until the peep lines up with your line of sight.

Method 2: Twist or Untwist the String – This achieves alignment by adjusting the number of twists in the string. This usually requires only a couple of twists.

1. Put the bow in the bow press and relax the string enough so you can remove it from the peg on the side of the cam or from the teardrop.

2. Add 1 complete twist to the string. (A complete twist is necessary to keep the string bending in the same direction.) Twist or untwist the string, depending on 1) the direction and 2) how much the peep turns.

3. Put the string back on the peg/teardrop, remove it from the bow press, and check it.

4. Repeat as necessary to get the hole in the peep aligned with the line of sight.

Properly installed, the peep should not rotate more than 1/8 turn. If it does, it may sit differently in different temperatures, as string material is somewhat temperature sensitive. In general, a lot of rotation indicates the string is not properly set up.

There are two things you can do to correct a lot of rotation. 1) Remove all the twists of the string and put the same number of twists in the opposite direction. 2) The direction of the serving affects the direction the string rotates, so reserve the center serving in the opposite direction. (See Chapter 7.)

Once the peep is close to proper position, recheck the vertical position if you weren't able to see through it. If you move it vertically, it may be necessary to do a little more adjustment of the rotation afterward.

When it is correctly positioned both vertically and with rotation, do the final step – serve it in place.

Serve the Peep in Place

This keeps the peep in place when you shoot. There are a couple methods for this, also.

Method 1: Do a Serving – With serving thread, do a short *Start a Serving* and *Finish a Serving* both above and below the peep. This will permanently position it. Starting and Finishing a Serving is discussed in Chapter 6.

Method 2: Tie a Moveable Knot – This uses Method 1 of 'Serving on a Nocking Point,' putting serving above and below the peep, described in Chapter 9. Like the nocking point, it leaves a way to slightly readjust the vertical position of the peep.

Once you have the peep in place, measure from the peep to the nocking point and record it with other information you have on your bow setup. This will save time the next time you set up a new string.

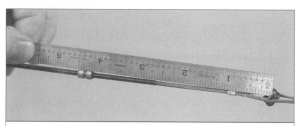

For a reference when setting up another string, measure the distance from the peep to the nocking point.

Chapter 12
Installing a Kisser Button

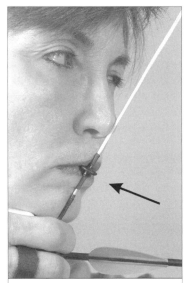

The kisser button touches the lips and provies an additional reference for the anchor.

A kisser button got its name because it touches the lips – you 'kiss' it. By adding an additional reference point, it helps maintain a consistent anchor.

The shape of your face may or may not allow you to use a kisser button effectively. A large nose along with a somewhat strong jaw may keep your lips from coming anywhere near the kisser button, no matter how large it is. So take your facial structure into consideration.

And just touching the lips is not ideal, because skin and flesh easily move. It's better to touch the kisser button to a tooth while maintaining the head position. Some compromise is often necessary, because the extra reference point changes the head position a little.

There are a number of different styles of kisser buttons, varying in size, shape, and how they are held in place. Most have a sleeve that fits around the string and a disc of some sort perpendicular to the string. One type of kisser is clamped on the string with nock sets.

Note: To serve a kisser button, you must be comfortable with beginning a serving and ending a serving, as described in Chapter 6. This serving requires a little more dexterity, so some practice with just starting and ending the serving is recommended before attempting to add a kisser button.

Installing a kisser button requires some materials.
- The kisser button
- Thin serving thread, ideally on a serving jig.
- A pair of scissors
- A bow square or ruler to make a reference mark

Getting the Kisser Button onto the String

Depending on the type of kisser button, this can be easy or a real pain. You must get all the strands of the string inside the sleeve, strand by strand. If you're lucky, several will go at one time.

1. On a recurve bow, have the bow un-strung with the string in position ready for stringing – the upper loop of the string is over the upper limb and the lower loop isin the string groove on the end of the limb. This gives you some force to get the strands into the sleeve.

   Several strands inside sleeve.

   On a compound, it may be possible to bend the kisser up-down (as it would be on the string) and put it on the string. Otherwise, it is necessary to relax the bow in a bow press.

2. Separate the strands of the string and select one or two.

3. While pulling the string against the string groove on the lower limb, slide one or several strands, if possible, through the slot in the kisser. Be sure the strand(s) are completely within the sleeve before attempting the next one(s).

4. Repeat this until all strands are inside the sleeve. Move the kisser up and down the string to test it.

Occasionally the sleeve is too small to hold all the strands. A different kisser button may have a larger sleeve, or if the string is really thick, it may not be possible. *All the strands must be within the sleeve.*

Once the bow string is completely inside the sleeve of the kisser button, string the bow or remove it from the press. Then determine where it should be positioned and serve it in place.

Determining the Position

If you are trying a kisser button for the first time, determine where to place it. Most of the time the kisser fits snugly enough on the string that you can push it up and down and will stay where pushed. If it's loose, develop a way to temporarily keep it from moving until you know where it should be. This could be putting a nocking point locator lightly on the string below the kisser (so you can slide it), or possibly doing a small serving which can be moved.

1. Move the kisser button close to where it should be on the string.

2. Using your tab or release, draw the bow with an arrow (pointing at a target to be safe!) and check the feel of the kisser against the lips at full draw.

3. Let down and move the kisser button if it needs repositioning.

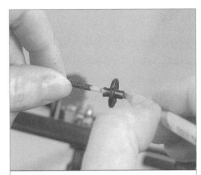

4. Repeat steps 2-3 until it is comfortably between the lips or properly touching a tooth. It may take several tries.

5. Once you know where it should be, mark the string with a pencil on the bottom and top edges of the sleeve. You'll need both marks to be sure the kisser is in the correct position when serving.

Marking the location of the kisser button on the string. Use a pencil and mark both sides.

Serving the Kisser Button in Place

Serving permanently attaches the kisser button on the string. While there are other ways to attach a kisser button, the methods described here virtually guarantee the kisser button won't move during shooting.

Note: If your kisser button uses nock sets around the sleeve, simply clamp them tight. While this usually works at least reasonably well with most strings, the kisser may not stay in place on a thin string.

The Conceptual Procedure – Once the kisser button is on the string, decide how it needs to be served before starting. For all, when done, it should fit snugly on the string.

This procedure puts one or two layers of serving above and below the kisser, extending about 1/2" from it. Where you start and the direction the wraps move in relation to the kisser depends on the fit of the kisser on the string.

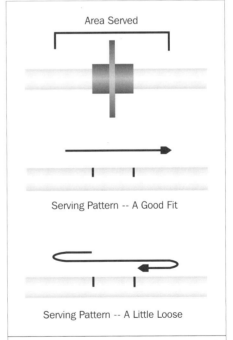

Serving patterns. A Good Fit needs only one layer of serving above and below; a Little Loose needs two. If the kisser has a Lot of Wobble, serve a layer of thin serving thread over the whole area first, slide the kisser onto it and serve as a Good Fit.

Take a look at how tightly the sleeve fits the string. There are three types of fit, depending on the size of the string and the size of the sleeve.

Good Fit – If the kisser fits the string snugly with no lateral give or wobble, you need only *Start a Serving* on one end, serve to the kisser, and *Finish a Serving* on the other side.

A Little Loose – If the kisser is a little loose, *Start a Serving* at a mark, serve away from it, then return, which adds a layer of serving on top of the one already there. Then pass through the kisser and repeat this – serve away from the kisser and *Finish a Serving* on top of that layer.

A Lot of Wobble – If the sleeve is too large for the string and it wobbles in place, before serving the kisser, first add a layer of thin serving the entire length where the kisser will be served, including the area of the string that will covered by the serving. Slide the kisser on to this. The kisser should then have a Good Fit.

Note: 1) Even though you are using a serving jig, it only holds the serving thread. All wraps are done by hand.

2) The wraps of the serving thread should be tight, usually a little tighter than those needed for a center serving.

The Procedure – The kisser button should be on the string and a recurve bow should be strung.

Note: The terms **Good Fit** and a **Little Loose** are used throughout to identify what to do in each situation. A Lot of Wobble assumes you have an additional layer served onto the string, so follow Good Fit.

1. For a **Good, Fit**, *Start a Serving* about 1/2" from one mark made for the position of the kisser. For a **Little Loose**, start at the mark.

2. Tightly wrap the serving by hand for about 1/2".
   Good Fit: To the mark
   Little Loose: Away from the mark.

3. [Skip this for Good Fit] For a **Little Loose**, after the initial 1/2", reverse direction and serve over the serving just laid down, towards where the kisser will be. This brings you back to the mark.

Good Fit: Start the Serving about 1/2" from the kisser mark.

4. Slide the kisser button to the serving, and apply light pressure to see if the sleeve will sit at the mark. Some-times the end of the sleeve moves over the serving a little, making the position a little different than intended. If that happens, add enough wraps to position it properly.

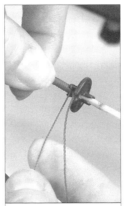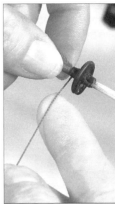

Kisser slides over the end of the serving, so the position is off.	Extra wraps put the kisser in proper position.

5. With the kisser button in the place, take the serving thread up through the slot in the kisser. Another 1/2" of serving needs to be added on the other side of the kisser.

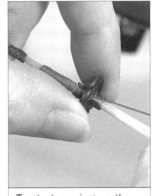

6. [Skip this for Good Fit] For a **Little Loose,** serve about 1/2"on the other side of the kisser, making sure the beginning of this serving holds the kisser in place. You may have to push the serving under the kisser a little.

To start serving on the other side, put the thread through the slot.

7. For a **Good Fit,** *Finish the Serving*, making the final wraps go away from the kisser to create about 1/2" of serving. To start the final wrapping, put the serving thread coming from the jig through the slot in the kisser. This makes it easier to serve. Make sure the initial wraps are tight against the kisser.

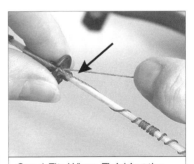

For a **Little Loose,** count the number of wraps, add a couple, and *Finish the Serving*, moving back over the serving already on the string, towards the kisser.

Good Fit: When *Finishing the Serving*, take the end of the serving coming from the jig back through the slot before starting the wraps. The thread being held will wrap over this.

For either, make sure there are enough wraps so the kisser button is held snugly on the string.

8. Trim the end.

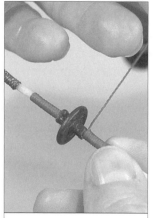

Installation of kisser button complete.

Once you know the kisser button is set correctly, it is a good idea to measure the distance between the kisser and the nocking point and mark your bow square. When building the next string, you have a reference point for positioning it.

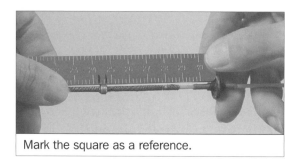

Mark the square as a reference.

You may need to check your sight marks. Kisser buttons rarely end up in exactly the same position. Your sight marks will be close, but may not be exact.

Chapter 13
Waxing the String

Wax protects the string from abrasion and moisture. Some string materials have a lot of wax; others have little or none. While all strings can use a little wax, strings with little or no wax need some protection, particularly if there is a possibility of rain.

Waxing a string serves several purposes – it helps lubricate the string fibers, it keeps the fibers from absorbing moisture, and it helps hold the strands together. As the wax rubs off from contact with your armguard or clothing protector, the string fibers will fray and become fuzzy. This makes the string more vulnerable to wear. So periodically the wax needs to be replaced.

String wax is not the same as the paraffin used in candles – it is a little gummy. It is available at almost any archery shop, so it's a good idea to keep a tube handy. The only disadvantage of storing it in your tackle box is if it's hot (in your car, on the field) – wax melts!

When waxing the string, you need to work the wax into the fibers.

1. String the bow if it isn't already strung.

2. Along the string fibers, rub the wax against the string in a lengthwise motion, applying the wax evenly and sparingly. Apply more in the frayed areas. *Do not wax the servings.*

3. Work the wax into the string by first rubbing it along its length with your fingers. Done fast enough, your fingers generate a little heat, helping the wax penetrate the string fibers.

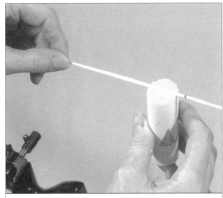

Apply the wax lightly to the string except where there is serving.

4. To really work the wax into the string, roll the string between your thumb and fingertips. Add more wax if needed.

Rolling the string between the fingertips helps the wax penetrate the string figers.

Part III: Working with Sights

These are easy things you can do to make sure your sight is properly set in relation to the bow.

First some terminology. The sight has a number of different parts, so the discussions in this section use the following terms. Every sight is different, so determine if yours is similar or simpler, and possibly where some pieces are combined.

Mount Block – Screwed into the bow, it holds the extension.

Extension – Attached to the mount block, it holds the sight bar out from the bow. On inexpensive sights, this is often combined with the mount block.

Sight Bar – The vertical piece held out from the bow by the extension. It almost always has a scale of some sort to make it easier to determine the correct position of the sight block for different distances.

Sight Block – The piece that rides on the sight bar. It is adjustable for different distances. Any moderate to high-end sight block has an easy way to adjust the sight pin left or right. That is the windage adjustment. Better quality sights have a micro-adjustment knob for this.

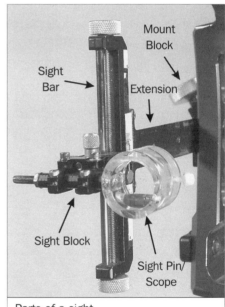

Parts of a sight.

Sight Pin/Scope – Held in the sight block, it is the piece you look at/through when shooting. On a target compound it is a scope, on a target recurve, it is usually a ring or something similar. On a hunting bow, often there are a set of pins instead of a single sight block, mounted directly on the sight bar. They are adjusted individually.

On sights, you can make the following simple adjustments to get better or more accurate performance from your bow.

Chapter 14
Getting More Distance on the Sight Bar

This is important for recurve shooters, but may be useful for any lighter draw weight bow with a sight. It becomes important when shooting longer distances, because the sight pin needs to come down as far as possible and allow clearance for the arrow fletching.

New sights almost always have the extension mounted in the middle of the sight bar, and the sight certainly can be used without changing it. However, even with the sight block as far down as it will go on the sight bar, there may still be a substantial distance between the sight pin and the arrow. By moving the sight bar down a set of holes that are drilled on the back of the bar, you can effectively gain distance on your sight.

Note: One thing to check.before starting this procedure. Move the sight block as far down on the sight bar as possible, then nock an arrow. If the distance between the sight pin and the arrow is less than 1/2", the fletching may strike the sight pin on the shot. In this case, there is no point to lowering the sight bar.

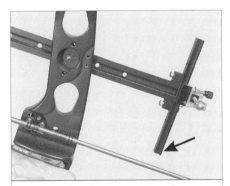

The sight bar is centered on the extension, keeping the sight block from moving down as far as it could and limiting the distance possible.

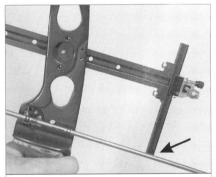

With the bar lower, the sight block can come further down. This allows more distance on the sight bar without moving the extension inward.

Note: Before doing this, read Chapter 15. After moving the sight bar, you will need to align it to the string. Both these procedures use the same screws, and you can do both at one time.

1. Remove the sight from the bow and the sight block from the sight bar so you have just the extension and the sight bar.

2. On the back of the sight bar, note how many holes are visible above the extension mount.

3. Remove the screws that hold the sight bar to the extension. The sight bar should come free.

4. Remount the extension in the *next highest set of holes* on the sight bar. This moves the sight bar down.

5. Replace the sight block on the sight bar and put the sight on the bow.

Some but not all better quality sights have calibrated the ruler on the sight bar so match the distance the sight bar moves, so you don't have to resight all your distances; instead, just move them up one large unit.

Chapter 15
Aligning the Sight Bar to the String

The sight bar must be vertical regardless of whether the bow is vertical. If it isn't, the arrows will move left or right on the target as you change distances, requiring windage adjustment for every distance.

Almost all competitive target shooters use a sight, whether compound or recurve, and hold the bow vertical. So an easy way to make sure the sight is vertical is to make the sight bar parallel to the string. All better-quality sights have an adjustment for this.

If you're not familiar with parts of a sight, see the introduction to this section on sights. They are labeled there.

The sight bar is almost always attached to some horizontal piece by two screws, whether a true extension or not. The hole for one of these screws is either slotted rather than round or a larger round hole. Either allows some left-right adjustment of one end of the sight bar.

The larger hole on the top allows left-right adjustment of that end of the sight bar.

Note: If you shoot a recurve bow, read Chapter 14 before starting. You may also want to reposition the sight bar on the extension, and it's better to do that first. Doing it after aligning the sight bar will require redoing this, since both use the same screws.

To make this adjustment, you need the following materials/tools.
- Your strung bow with the sight mounted
- A ruler or something of similar length and width
- A screw driver, hex wrench, etc., that matches the screws that hold the sight bar on the extension.

1. The sight bar sits behind the sight window out of view, so you need to extend the edge of the bar to see both it and the string at the same time. This is what the ruler is for. Lay the edge of the ruler along the sight bar *from end to end*. Re-

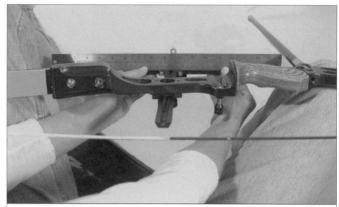

The ruler against the sight bar extends the edge of the bar out beyond the sight window. Be sure the edge sits on the entire length of the bar.

move the sight block if necessary.

2. Visually line up the edge of the ruler with the string and look carefully at each end. Properly aligned, the string should appear to touch the edge of the ruler. Allow for the thickness of the center serving when looking at this.

3. If it isn't in line, *slightly* loosen both screws that hold the sight bar, leaving enough pressure on them so the sight bar moves smoothly; it doesn't flop around.

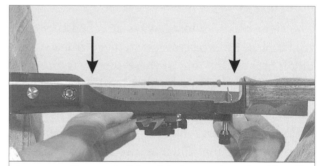

Improper alignment of the sight bar to the string. Visually, the ruler is not touching the string on both ends.

4. Determine which screw has the slotted/larger hole by moving both ends of the sight bar.

5. Shift the end of the sight bar with the slotted/larger hole to align the sight bar with the string. This is very precise, and a small move makes a

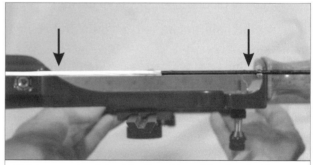

Sight properly aligned to the string. Allowing for the width of the serving, the string touches the ruler along its entire length.

large difference, so check the alignment with the ruler a number of times.

6. Once aligned, tighten the end with the round hole first, then the slotted/ larger hole. This helps keep the sight bar in position. It may be good to do this in increments – tighten both screws a little, then check the alignment, and tighten again, etc. This is a fine adjustment, so the smallest shift throws the whole thing off (as could occur with the pressure of the screw against the sight bar as it is tightened).

7. Check the alignment one more time, as tightening the screws may have shifted the sight bar.

If you consistently cant the bow (tip it off vertical) and want to shoot that way, the sight bar must still be vertical. (As said before, if the sight isn't vertical, your windage will change whenever you change distances.) In this situation, the sight bar will be angled in relation to the bow, but it will be vertical when you're shooting.

Getting it vertical will take some experimentation. Most likely the adjustment needed will be beyond the range of adjustment designed for the sight, so devise another method of first holding the sight bar vertical and then keeping it in place.

Chapter 16
Leveling the Scope Level

There are two groups of compound sights – those with one or more fixed pins mounted on the vertical sight bar and those with a single scope mounted in a sight block that moves on the sight bar. The first type is predominately for hunting and those divisions simulating hunting; the second type is commonly used by target shooters.

The level on a compound scope needs to be leveled to be sure the bow is vertical when shooting.

On a compound, the target sight almost always is a magnifying scope with a level. The level indicates vertical when shooting, avoiding left-right errors. But if it is not vertically in line with the bow, it needs to be leveled. Leveling the scope level will keep the bow vertical when you shoot uphill, downhill, or on flat ground, so your group will stay centered.

Thre are two ways to do this. The first uses a leveler, a piece designed for this. The second allows you to level the level while the sight is on the bow. While it works, it is not as precise as the leveler.

Using the Leveler

To use a leveler, you need the following tools.
- A sight leveler. These can be purchased at most archery shops.
- A small level
- The wrenches that fit the screws holding the sight and scope

Set Up the Leveler – First get the leveler level in both the horizontal and vertical planes.

1. Attach the leveler to a solid surface.

2. Along both the horizontal and vertical planes, use the small level to be sure the leveler is level. Adjust it if necessary.

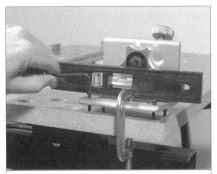

Leveling the leveler horizontally on the table. It must be mounted on a solid table so the leveler reads the sight level accurately.

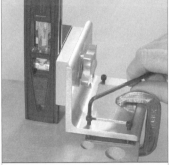

It also must be verticallly leveled. This must be done before working with the scope bubble.

Level the Scope Level – There are two planes to level. As you look at the sight, the first is left-right; the other is front-back rotation of the bow, as would happen shooting up and downhill.

1. Attach the sight to the leveler.

2. Place a small level against the side of the sight bar and use the adjustments on it to level the sight bar. You may need to remove the sight block from the sight bar to do this.

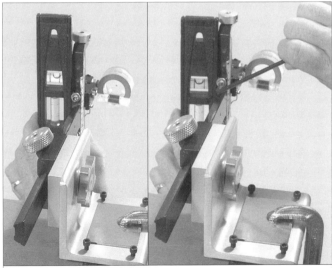

Getting the sight vertical. The adjustment screws are on the back of the sight bar.

3. If you removed the sight block, put it back on the sight bar and adjust the scope until it is level. How to do this varies on different sights; there should be an adjustment on the sight block. Check the manufacturer's instructions, too.

| The bubble is not centered even though the sight is vertical. | Use the adjustment on the sight block to center the bubble. |

4. Move the sight leveler up to a 45° angle and readjust the scope to level.

5. Then move it down to a 45° angle and readjust the scope again.

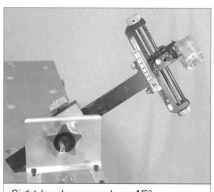

Sight leveler moved up 45°.

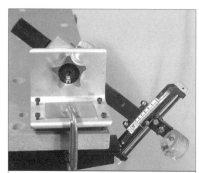

Sight leveler moved down 45°.

6. Repeat Steps 3-5 until it shows level at all three positions.

7. Reattach the sight to the bow. It is ready to shoot.

The sight leveled and ready to shoot.

Leveling the Level with the Sight on the Bow

If you do not have a leveler, you can achieve most of this working with the sight on the bow. While this works, it is not as precise as the leveler.

There are only three tools you need.
- A worktable and a way to mount the bow
- A small level
- The wrenches that fit the screws on the sight and scope.

1. Clamp the bow to something solid that will keep the scope bubble steady.

2. Make sure the string is vertical. If necessary, readjust the bow position.

The moveable surface of this worktable holds the bow.

Adjusting the bow so the string is vertical.

3. Align the sight bar to the string as described in Chapter 15, or being sure the string (bow) stays vertical, make the sight bar vertical. Use the screws on the back of the sight bar.

Making the sight bar vertical. The string must be vertical, too.

4. Note the position of the scope bubble. If it is not centered, it needs to be leveled. Make the adjustment on the sight block. How this is done is different for each sight brand, but look for the adjustment on the sight block. Follow the manufacturer's information.

The bubble needs to be in the center of the level.	Making the adjustment to level the scope and level.

The sight pin is now leveled and ready to shoot.

The level scope.

Chapter 17
Centering the Sight Pin

This is primarily for target sights with a single sight pin, whether a scope on a compound or a unmagnified sight on a recurve. This discussion refers to specific parts of the sight, so if you are unfamiliar with the parts of the sight, review the information at the beginning of this Part (Part III: Working with Sights).

In the discussion that follows, all target sights have a piece which holds the sight pin and is inserted into or attached to the sight block. The exact configuration of these varies from sight to sight, so examine yours closely. On most older sights, it was round. On newer high-end sights, it may be square or some other shape. Whatever its shape, in these discussions, it is called the *holder*.

Sight blocks vary in how the holder'holds the sight pin. On the left, two hex nuts on the sides of the odd-shped holder hold the pin. On the right, there is a square Holder inside the sight block. The screw within the open slot on the front of the sight pin locks the pin in place.

In general, it is best to have the sight pin near the center of the range allowed for windage adjustment. That way, you have latitude for adjustment in difficult conditions like wind or rain. If you have a new sight, you can set the windage while keeping the holder centered in the adjustment range. After shooting a while, if the adjustment is all the way to one side, it needs to be recentered. Doing either is easy.

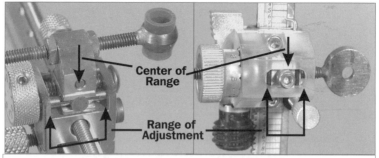

Two sight blocks centered within the range allowed for windage adjustment.

Setting the Windage on a New Sight

When you are ready to shoot a new sight, follow this procedure to initially set the windage in the center of the adjustment range.

1. If necessary, recenter the holder with the micro-adjustment knob as you would normally do when shooting. New sights generally have the windage adjustment centered within the range allowed, but check it to be sure.

2. Loosen the screw(s)/nut(s) that hold the sight pin in the holder. The location of these varies from sight to sight, so look for how yours is held in the holder. They may be visible when the sight is assembled, or (mostly on older sights) it may be necessary to partially or completely remove the holder from the sight block to find the set screws in it.

3. Shoot, adjusting the windage by turning the sight pin in the sight block. If it was necessary to remove the holder from the sight block, you'll have to do this in stages, moving the sight pin, assembling the sight block again, shooting and seeing if it's on center, then adjusting it again if necessary. Luckily, you'll only do this once!

4. Once sighted in, tighten the screw(s)/nut(s) to hold the sight pin in place. From now on, use the micro adjustment for minor changes in windage.

Recentering the Windage

If the micro-adjustment is all the way to one side of the range allowed for windage, it can be recentered without losing the windage setting.

1. Recenter the holder within the adjustment range, using the micro-adjustment knob and *counting the number of full turns needed to move it to center.*

2. Loosen the screw(s)/nut(s) that hold the sight pin in place. Remember, where these are located vary. They may be visible when the sight is assembled for shooting, or on older sights you may have to partially or completely remove the holder from the sight block to find the set screws.

3. Turn the sight pin the same number of turns *in the opposite direction*. This returns it to the initial windage setting. If you are adjusting this because you need to move the sight pin farther, add the additional turns after recentering the pin.)

4. Tighten the locking screw(s)/nut(s) and reassemble the sight block, if necessary.

Chapter 18
Changing a Sight Pin without Losing the Windage

If you've been shooting a while, most likely the windage for the sight pin is set correctly. At some point, if you decide to try a different sight pin and don't have a second sight block, the windage setting is lost when you remove the pin. This procedure allows you to change the sight pin and at least be in the 'ballpark' for the windage setting so you don't miss the target the first time you shoot with it.

Like Chapter 17, this is for sights with a single sight pin, whether a scope or an unmagnified pin for a recurve, where there the holder holds the pin. (If you are unfamiliar with the parts of a sight, see the information at the beginning of this Part – Part III: Working with Sights).

There are couple ways to save the windage setting without having to sight in again. While it may not be pinpoint accurate, either methods gets the new pin close. For one, you need a small ruler, the other uses a piece of wood or stiff cardboard.

Method 1 - Using a Ruler for Measurement

1. Remove the sight block from the sight bar. It's just easier to work that way.

2. Measure the distance from the side of the sight block to the center of the sight pin. The ruler must sit against a part of the block *that does not move* if the windage is adjusted.

Measuring the distance from the side of the sight block to the center of the sight pin.

Measuring to the center is necessary because sight pins vary in diameter, and unless the new pin is exactly the same diameter as the old one, the distance to the edge will be different.

3. To get the new sight pin in the ballpark, note the distance of the edge of the sight pin from the edge of the holder.

4. Remove the holder from the sight block and the sight pin from the holder.

5. Replace the sight pin in the holder with the new pin, setting the pin to the distance described in Step 3.

6. Using the micro-adjustment knob, set the windage to the center of the adjustment range.

7. By turning the pin (*do not use the micro-adjustment*), position the pin the same distance from the sight block as measured in Step 2. Be sure the ruler touches the same place on the sight block as it did when you measured it.

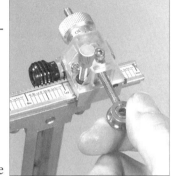

8. Shoot, making any further adjustments in the windage by moving the sight pin. Again, *do not move the micro-adjustment.* This sets the windage for the middle of the adjustment range. When the group is in the middle, tighten the screw(s)/nut(s) to lock the sight pin in place.

When installing the new sight pin, set the initial windage by turning the pin, not the microadjustment.

Once you have the sight pin adjusted so the bow shoots on center, use the windage micro-adjustment knob for minor changes during shooting.

Method 2 – Using a Block of Wood for Measurement

This method works better for scopes on compounds, as there is no hole to mark the center through. You need a piece of wood, stiff cardboard, or anything rigid that can be marked. However, something that has some depth (like wood) is generally better, because it is easier to hold it against the sight block.

1. Remove the sight block from the sight bar.

2. Place the block of wood against the side of the sight block. It should touch an area that does not move when the windage is adjusted.

3. Mark the wood for the center of the pin, through the hole and/or above and below it.

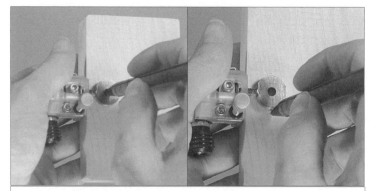

Marking the position of the sight pin. Through the hole works on many recurve sight pins, but above and below is better for a scope.

4. Remove the holder from the sight block and the pin from the holder.

5. Install the new pin and replace the holder in the sight block.

6. Set the micro-adjustment to the center of the adjustment range.

7. Using the marks on the block of wood, turn the sight pin until the center is in the same position as the old one. (Do not use the microadjustment). *Be sure the block of wood sits against the sight block exactly the way it did when you marked it.*

8. Place the sight block back on the sight bar.

9. Shoot, initially adjusting the windage by turning the sight pin, not using the micro-adjustment.

Turn the new sight pin until the center of the pin lines up the reference marks.

10. When the group is centered, lock the sight pin in place. After this, use the microadjustment for minor changes.

About the Authors

Alan Anderson is a long-time archer and a meticulous craftsman. Whether making bow strings, building airplanes or crafting close-up magic illusions, Alan is in his element working with his hands and paying attention to detail. He took up archery in the early 1970s and was an active shooter well into the 1980s. After a long sabbatical to raise a family and earn a living he returned to archery in 1997. He holds an NAA Level 2 Archery Instructor certificate and enjoys competition. Alan lives with his wife and two daughters (all archers) in Northern Virginia.

Ruth Rowe is an Olympian, coach, technical writer, producer, and a life-long archer. She is well known in the archery community and has traveled the world representing the United States in archery competitions since the early 1970s. Ruth owns an impressive list of competition wins including the 1983 Pan American Championship, multiple National indoor and outdoor championships, state and regional championships, field championships, and she has set multiple archery world records. The US Olympic Committee named her Sportswoman of the year for Archery in 1983 and she represented the United States in the 1984 Olympic Games.

Ruth's first book, *Fundamentals of Recurve Target Archery* and her instructional videos, *Archery: The Basics* and *Archery: Refining Your Form* set the standard for recurve archery training and are sold world-wide. She is active in the National Archery Association as a member of the National Governing Board and the Coach's Development Committee. Ruth writes, teaches, and coaches in Northern Virginia.

Publications Available from Quintessential Corporation

Fundamentals of Recurve Target Archery
Archery: The Basics (video)
Archery: Refining Your Form (video)

Future Publications

Fundamentals of Compound Target Archery
Moving Up: Improving Your Recurve Skills
Moving Up: Improving Your Compound Skills
A Coach's Assistant

Simple Maintenance for Archery

Easy things you can do
to maintain your equipment

Ruth Rowe

Alan Anderson

ISBN 0-9715298-1-7

Quintessential Productions
www.qproductsarchery.com